P9-CAO-272

Making Love During Pregnancy

Making Love During Pregnancy

by Elisabeth Bing and Libby Colman

Drawings by David Passalacqua

BANTAM BOOKS
TORONTO · NEW YORK · LONDON · SYDNEY

Acknowledgments

We want to thank the many parents who made this book a reality. It was through their wonderfully frank and personal accounts that we could put this book together. We are also very grateful to Dr. Lawrence Jackman, Director of the Division of Human Sexuality, Department of Obstetrics and Gynecology of the Albert Einstein College of Medicine, for his invaluable help in making research material, as well as some of the letters from his patients, available to us.

Elisabeth Bing
Libby Colman

MAKING LOVE DURING PREGNANCY
A Bantam Book/October 1977

All rights reserved.
Copyright © 1977 by Elisabeth Bing and Libby Colman.
Illustrations Copyright © 1977 by Bantam Books, Inc.

This book may not be reproduced in whole or in part, by mimeograph or any other means, without permission.
For information address: Bantam Books, Inc.

ISBN   0-553-01396-3

Published simultaneously in the United States and Canada

Bantam Books are published by Bantam Books, Inc. Its trademark, consisting of the words "Bantam Books" and the portrayal of a rooster, is Registered in U.S. Patent and Trademark Office and in other countries. Marca Registrada. Bantam Books, Inc., 666 Fifth Avenue, New York, New York 10103.

PRINTED IN THE UNITED STATES OF AMERICA

12   11   10   9   8   7   6   5   4   3

Contents

Preface

Until recently, sex during pregnancy was a taboo subject. Traditional obstetrics observed the law of silence on this matter. Conditioned by tradition and alienated by convention, both the pregnant woman and her husband did not dare to discuss making love during pregnancy, although both thought about it. It was only after the work of Masters and Johnson, W. Pasini, and myself had achieved worldwide acceptance that the veil was lifted and couples began at last to feel liberated from their inhibitions.

In this excellent book, my friend Elisabeth Bing and her colleague, Libby Colman, succeed in removing the mystery that has always surrounded the feelings and events of pregnancy. Through detailed studies of couples facing pregnancy, they demonstrate that sex during pregnancy can be fulfilling for both husband and wife. They show, too, how the husband can be entirely involved in his wife's pregnancy from the moment of conception to the birth of the child. Through a continued, shared experience of sex during these nine months, a couple begins to define in a context of mutual trust and love their individual responsibilities toward the child they will have together.

In my book, **Childbirth Without Pain,** I hoped to provide couples with an education of the prenatal state in order to give them a better under-standing of the changes in a woman's body throughout pregnancy. Sexual behavior during pregnancy was particularly emphasized so that every couple could gain a new perspective on the experience of pregnancy and birth.

At long last, the father is being allowed in the delivery room. He can now understand his pater-nity with as much clarity and pride as his wife views her motherhood. As a result, men today accept responsibility more readily on the basis of this par-ticipation. And, as a witness, the father can assess qualities until then unknown to him in his own wife: energy, self-control, will. The bond between the couple is reinforced. The father will accept the newcomer to the family more willingly. A triangular relationship which is very favorable to the child is thus established at the outset.

From the moment that child care begins, the father now **feels** himself to be the father, having shared so intimately in the process of creation. The nursing period will no longer be lived through by the father as a time of frustration and the resump-tion of sexual relations between man and wife, if they were interrupted during the postpartum period, will occur with a greater degree of under-standing and sensitivity on the part of the father, who, having witnessed the birth of his child, will better understand the changes in his wife's body. The sexual dialogue that began during pregnancy will continue, to the great benefit of the couple. Finally, it is striking to observe that in the accounts quoted in this book, the word "we" is always used.

The excellent work done by the two authors of this book should make people more aware of the importance of a couple jointly experiencing pregnancy. They have examined an aspect of pregnancy which the medical profession is beginning to view with great importance, that is, that pregnancy and the birth of a child brings into play the sexuality of a woman, her husband, and, ultimately, has a profound effect on the marriage relationship itself.

I thank them and am very happy to have the privilege of writing the preface of this work.

Dr. Pierre Vellay

Secretary General of the International Society for Preventive Psychological and Obstetrical Medicine

Author of **Childbirth Without Pain** and
Childbirth With Confidence

Paris
November 20, 1976

Introduction

The idea of putting this book together came to us two or three years ago. It was a time when Americans had become aware of the need for frank discussion on the formerly taboo subject of human sexuality. Masters and Johnson were household words. People seemed less inhibited than they had been before. At the same time, more and more information was available about another formerly taboo subject, pregnancy and childbirth. But there was still little or no information available discussing sex in relation to the changes of pregnancy. It was as though the new freedom made possible by effective contraception had created a split between sex and pregnancy, and the two could not be discussed together except for "family planning."

As a childbirth instructor in the Lamaze method who has trained thousands of couples over many years, and as a writer and lecturer whose focus has been on pregnancy and the family, we were seeing that many couples did not understand the changes in their bodies and in their relationships that took place during and after pregnancy. While they continued to love each other as much, they found that the physical expression of that love was altered—sometimes distressingly so—and each couple thought that its own problems were unique. They had nowhere to go for help or reas-

1

surance in these very intimate matters. Even in our liberated age, people are confused about whether or not it is all right to make love in pregnancy.

Although it may seem that people became interested in this subject only recently, there has been concern with the subject of making love in pregnancy in earlier generations. In 1918 the well-known writer and physician, Dr. Marie Stopes, who specialized in problems of family life wrote:

> Much has been written, and may be found in the innumerable books on the sex-problem, as to whether a man and a woman should or should not have relations while the wife is bearing an unborn child. In this matter experience is very various, so that it is difficult or impossible to give definite advice without knowing the full circumstances of each case. I have heard from a number of women that they desire union urgently at this time; while to others the thought of it is incredible.[1]

Decades later, this confusion is still with us. We too have heard contradictory evidence and spoken with people who have had opposite experiences. The only common denominators in any talk on sexual behavior during pregnancy and immediately after birth seem to be a lack of knowledge and a hesitancy to discuss sex with the doctor or obstetrician. Even in cases when sex was discussed, answers were inconsistent, frequently quite arbitrary, and seemed to have little or no relation to the needs and desires of the individuals.

Therefore, we asked ourselves how we could proceed with a book that would be a meaningful guide to men and women during their childbearing years, when their needs and attitudes are so varied.

We reviewed the popular literature; it rarely, if ever, touched on sexuality during pregnancy. To find out medical opinion, we studied older and also more recent papers written in the professional literature, to see what kind of research had actually been done. And finally we asked young couples who had come for childbirth-preparation classes to write down their thoughts, their experiences, their joys, their anxieties, and especially their feelings on making love during pregnancy and after the birth of their child.

Dr. Stopes followed a similar procedure at the beginning of this century. She remarked:

> Far too few men and women are clean-minded and frank enough to record their feelings in this connection, and far too few medical men delicately sympathetic enough to elicit the facts, even from those women who are personally conscious of them. The accumulating evidence which I have acquired through direct personal confidences about this subject points in absolutely conflicting directions, and there is little doubt that in this particular, even more than in so many others, the health, needs, and mental condition of women who are bearing children vary profoundly.[2]

Advice on sexual behavior during this particular period in a couple's life is bound to be varied and dependent not only on medical observation, but also on individual circumstances. We have not set out to give medical advice in this book. Every couple should discuss sexual activities during

4

their pregnancy with their doctor; in fact, communication during this period is of utmost importance. It is our hope that after reading about the topic here, women will feel more comfortable discussing their particular situation with a helping professional. There cannot be hard and fast rules where human relations, personal emotions, sexual customs, and intimate behavior are concerned. Pregnancy is a time of personal upheaval for both men and women. Emotions go through rapid and intense changes, which often make it hard for husband and wife to keep in touch with each other's feelings. Because it is a time when they are setting out on a shared venture, it is particularly important that they stay close to each other and learn to be sensitive to each other's changing needs.

In this book, we want to present openly some of the prevalent feelings and ideas expressed by expectant parents today. We found that many couples would welcome an opportunity to talk about their own feelings and to learn more about sex during pregnancy and afterward. They would like a chance to talk about normal sexual behavior, desires, safety, and about a woman's changed body in relation to her lovemaking. They would like to be able to discuss this vital part of their lives before expectable changes grow into worries or problems. And yet they often do not seem to feel free to turn to their doctors.

One woman believed from her own limited experience with obstetricians and gynecologists, as well as from talks with friends, that the professionals almost categorically do not willingly help a woman with intimate problems. In her words: "After waiting one to two hours, you are raced through their office (albeit warmly) in five minutes,

6

and most women are either too embarrassed or too afraid to ask questions less they use up the doctor's 'valuable time.' " If she feels that way about doctors, where can she turn for help?

If a woman learns how to use her body during labor and delivery, if both she and her partner understand the normal changes of pregnancy and birth, whether physical or psychological, and if the couple wants to participate actively during the birth of their child, it seems logical to us that sex discussion should be an integral part of education for childbirth.

Unfortunately, such a program is rarely—if ever—offered to young couples. Medical literature is not readily available to them. Popular magazine articles generally offer such pleasant advice to the father as: "Just remember to be specially gentle and loving during the critical period." And, while obstetricians and doctors are quite willing to provide medical guidelines, they rarely have time for lengthy discussions on the psychological aspects of the question. Or perhaps the woman is reluctant to discuss her most intimate feelings with her physician. In any case, communication is often limited at best, and the father is frequently not included in the prenatal visits.

Attempts have been made to deal with some of these feelings in group or even individual therapy sessions, but we feel this avenue is not open to enough people, nor are such sessions necessarily indicated. The desire to understand more about ourselves and our relationships during childbearing should not be regarded as a pathological situation requiring treatment.

We wrote to approximately 200 to 300 couples and asked them to tell us of their experiences dur-

ing pregnancy, labor, and after the baby was born. We did not ask questions requiring specific answers, but gave loose guidelines to help couples jot down their thoughts and feelings. When replies started coming back, we realized that we received the most detailed reports from women and men who had happy sexual experiences during this period of their lives; we heard from those who felt that they would be able to adjust to the changes in their bodies, those who found new ways of pleasuring and caressing each other. We did not, however, get long reports from many who had unsatisfactory experiences for which they could find no solution, or who felt unhappy about their relationship with their partner during pregnancy. Therefore our accounts and quotes are mainly from happily married couples who enjoy sexual activity. We realize that there are many others who feel frustrated, deserted, who are alone, are single parents, or have unwanted pregnancies. There are also many couples who feel that intercourse is not a central element in their relationships.

It may be difficult for those women or men in special circumstances to identify with the people we have quoted. However, we think many of them will be able to find a way out of their own difficulties and frustrations through our pages.

As we read the experiences of men and women trying to cope with the changes in their lives, it became clear to us that we would never write a book with specific answers—dos or don'ts. We don't even feel that rigid rules should be supplied. These reports have revealed to us some widespread, almost universal beliefs, feelings, and thoughts which are sometimes medically founded—and sometimes not. They have also

9

shown us the unique response of each individual to the common changes experienced during the childbearing years. Each couple must seek its own solutions to the common problems.

Open discussion about feelings and a rational examination of fears should be possible for all. How easily we can make adjustments—and even laugh at ourselves—when we know we're not alone.

We have come to believe that this book represents one of the first steps toward the goal of honest exchange about making love during pregnancy. We hope that it will help clear the air and help men and women talk openly and frankly together about an area of human sexuality which still remains a closed subject, even in the sexually liberated 1970s.

The First Trimester

The moment of conception is the link between making love and the creation of a child. A few babies are made through artificial insemination. Some begin to grow after an act of sexual intercourse that had no element of love. But for many, conception occurs as only one moment in a long relationship between a man and a woman—a relationship in which sexual intercourse is only one of many manifestations of the love between them. That love has as much to do with the making of the child (and the environment in which he will grow) as does the single act which results in his conception.

Pregnancy adds many new elements to a loving relationship. The partners may have to subtly shift their ways of being together as they pass through the changes of pregnancy. That shift may even have begun before conception with the very decision to have a baby.

The decision often involves an active choice to stop previous contraceptive measures. This simple act can change the physical pleasure and emotional meaning of lovemaking. Sex may **gain** an extra level of excitement.

- **"From the time I stopped taking the Pill, our sex lives were altered—our relationship im-**

11

proved considerably. Whether this was due to the Pill itself, (or lack of it), or the anticipation of possible pregnancy, I don't know. I can say, however, that sex was delightful. We felt uninhibited, and somehow 'the pressure was off.' "

Since it usually takes a few months of trying before conceiving, and another few weeks before the pregnancy is confirmed, this period of playful work can extend for quite a while.

Even before the advent of the Pill, couples took joy in planning a baby. In 1877 a doctor gave this advice:

> If children are to be begotten . . . . the sexual embrace should be had in the light of the day. But it should not be the hurried act of the early morning, like a hasty meal before a day's work. As no function in life is more important, and as the consequences of a single act may be the happiness or misery of a future being, it is worth a little time and preparation. Indeed, it is impossible to name any function for the proper performance of which more elaborate preparation should be made. Yet it is almost the only one for which no preparation is usually made. Surely, if sexual intercourse is worth doing at all, it is worth doing well." [3]

Sometimes couples simply stop previous contraception and "let nature take its course." But modern couples can frequently and also fairly accurately predict when they are most likely to conceive because they can learn the use of basal thermometers, which will show the minute temperature changes that occur at ovulation time. Or they may have learned to use the fairly new "Billings method," which enables a woman to tell her ovulation period by the amount and density and consistency of her increased mucus discharge. Others may employ the less accurate rhythm method, which assumes that ovulation occurs within twelve to fourteen days after the first day of menstruation. In fact, couples who use effective contraceptive measures and then not only stop—but also try to detect ovulation time—actually transform conception from an accident into a purposeful and joyous act.

• **"When we saw the changes on the temperature chart, my husband called in to say he couldn't come to work. We went out for food and wine; then we spent the whole day together. After we made love, we opened a bottle of champagne and drank it right there in bed. We had quite a party."**

• **"Naturally we had a wonderful time trying to get pregnant. My husband would say, 'Just one more time to make sure.' "**

Not all couples who deliberately plan to create their child have an easy or joyous time of it. Women seldom ovulate during the first month after they stop taking the Pill. If they are not successful in the first few months, a couple may become anxious. All spontaneity seems to go out of lovemaking. Some men are not sure they are really ready to take on the responsibility of fatherhood and become impotent in response to making love on demand. Some women begin to feel sex is a dreary

13

bore, a chore bereft of personal pleasure. But for those who have had to work hard to conceive, the moment of triumph can be great indeed. Relaxed lovemaking can feel like a newfound pleasure.

- **"We had been trying to get pregnant for six to nine months before I conceived, and it got to be like a stud farm those last few months. So that when I was pregnant the pressure to have sex, per se, was gone and we were so much more relaxed and happy to just 'screw' whenever and however we wanted."**

- **"For nearly four years we'd been on a strict schedule of abstinence/performance, and I can testify that it had not been anything like a picnic. An extra bonus of finally becoming pregnant was not to have to make love by the calendar."**

- **"Our experience was that during the first trimester we both seemed to enjoy intercourse more than in the months preceding pregnancy, perhaps because we were no longer concerned with hitting the ovulatory period."**

Even today, not all pregnancies are the result of careful planning. Nevertheless they can have a good influence on lovemaking.

- **"I was not actively trying to become pregnant although we had switched to a less effective contraceptive method some months prior (from Pill to condom). We were letting chance play a more active role in the decision."**

14

- "During the first two months of pregnancy, I enjoyed sex actually more than previously. It's only fair to add, however, that (1) I didn't know I was pregnant, and (2) I was on vacation and therefore much more relaxed than usual."

- "When we found out I was pregnant, I felt even more like sex, and we had so much delight in the pregnancy that we had a lot to celebrate."

It is certainly ironic that a woman's greatest pleasure brought by the discovery that she is pregnant is the freedom from worry about whether or not she will get pregnant—but this is what couples report time and time again. There is more to this than just the joy of success. This new freedom to enjoy sex is almost as great for those who had been avoiding pregnancy as it is for those who had been working hard to become pregnant.

- "During the first trimester, my desire for sex seemed to increase. There was no more worrying about getting pregnant. Not that it was a worry for me, but my husband didn't really want me to get pregnant—probably because he felt we weren't financially stable to have a child at that time."

- "One pleasant aspect of pregnant sex was that I didn't have to get up to insert the diaphragm, which meant more spontaneity. Nor was I thinking, 'Will I get pregnant this time, or is it too early or late?' Sex during pregnancy is really sex totally separated from the possibility of pregnancy."

- "Sex during my pregnancy was even better than it was before I became pregnant. I felt mentally and physically freer. I didn't have to worry about birth control any more. I had many more desires than I did before, and because of this my husband's sexual appetite also grew! Sex was great! We both really let ourselves go."

- "Of course, one of the advantages of being pregnant is not having to worry about becoming pregnant and that in itself allows greater freedom sexually. In all my pregnancies I have found that my sex drive increased almost as soon as my first missed period and stayed that way up until my seventh or eighth month."

Freedom from contraception, however, is not always enough to make the experience of making love a joy in the early months of pregnancy; hormonal and physical changes occur the moment the sperm unites with the ovum. Many women could "sleep around the clock" during the first three months of their pregnancy. Even lovemaking may become too much of an effort. Others feel nauseous or even vomit not only in the mornings, but also in the evenings. Some become fearful that they might lose the baby when making love, some remember old wives' tales or have been told by friends that oxygen privation to the baby may occur when a woman has an orgasm. Often the father becomes anxious that he may hurt the baby through vigorous lovemaking. The joy in lovemaking is highly dependent on emotional factors. Anxieties and fears can easily frustrate a close and loving relationship.

18

- "Now that I've told you how relieved we were to be able to make love when we felt like it, let me add that I slept away the first trimester! My drive diminished—(all I wanted was sleep)—but once we got started, it seemed my nerve endings were more awake than ever."

- "During the first trimester of both my pregnancies, I experienced a great deal of nausea throughout the day. This definitely decreased my sexual desires. My green complexion and sickly state also tended to put a damper on my husband's ardor."

A woman who does not feel well enough to "make love"—that is, to participate in sexual intercourse—may enjoy a relaxing massage or just a back rub to help her feel loved and cared for through a difficult time. Sometimes it is enough just to be held and reassured that everything will be all right, that this nausea will not last forever. Physical closeness helps a couple share their joys and sorrows and stay in touch with each other's shifting needs. Extra cuddling and caressing can be gratifying to both parents during a time when their usual sexual relations are interrupted.

For most, the illness is a passing phenomena:

- "Except for the first three months when I felt sick constantly, sex was very enjoyable during pregnancy until the end. In fact it seemed particularly fulfilling to have both a baby and my husband inside of me. I feel close to my husband and excited by our relationship and the baby he has given me, so it would follow that sex remains good."

19

In addition to morning sickness and fatigue, there are other anxieties and fears which can make lovemaking difficult and undesirable early in pregnancy:

- **"For the first several months I was very unsexy—first of all because I didn't feel very well—fatigue, aches, and indigestion. Also, although I had read and been told by the doctor that there was no danger, I still had some fear that intercourse would cause miscarriage. Sexual desire has increased steadily after those first few months."**

The fear of miscarriage is common in the first few months of pregnancy even among women who have had no symptoms and no previous miscarriages. They often want to abstain from intercourse and/or from having orgasms because of this fear. If a woman has had spotting or has had a history of miscarriage, or is uncomfortable during intercourse, she is often told to abstain. A good doctor will be sure to indicate whether he wants her to abstain from intercourse, from orgasm, or from both. Orgasm may be seen as a potential cause of miscarriage in a woman with a sensitive uterus, for orgasms do cause the uterus to contract. Intercourse itself, that is, penetration of the penis into the vagina, does not usually cause contractions of the uterus. A deep thrust by the man may bring the penis up against the cervix, the mouth of the uterus. During pregnancy the cervix becomes softer than usual. There is so much extra blood in the vessels that pressure may cause a tiny bit of bleeding. Such bruises heal rapidly (they are roughly akin to a nose bleed) and can be avoided by using positions that avoid such deep penetration. If a woman has had no spotting and no history of miscarriage, her doctor will probably reassure her that she can relax and enjoy her usual forms of lovemaking.

Despite such reassurance, men and women continue to worry about it.

• "I never enjoyed sex during pregnancy as much as at other times. I found it more difficult to reach orgasm. Although I knew rationally that sex would not harm the baby, emotionally I felt it was a risk. I had two miscarriages between my first and second pregnancies, so when I became pregnant with my second child, I was nervous about doing anything which might affect the pregnancy. I'm sure the frequency of sex diminished."

It is interesting to notice that the fear of miscarriage diminished the pleasure and frequency of sexual relations but this woman continued to participate in sexual intercourse and had orgasms with no other adverse effects. Other women chose to abstain rather than worry and felt good about their decision:

• "The doctor I had for my first trimester urged no coitus the first three months. While I discarded other of his advice where I felt I had more updated or better information, I didn't dispute him here because I had never read anything to the contrary."

Many women report they make love in pregnancy to please their husbands even though they do not enjoy it themselves. It is unfortunate that such women cannot feel more free to communicate with their partners and find ways of expressing love that can give joy to both of them. If given a chance to express his feelings, it is likely that the husband also will say he feels his wife's unspoken reserve and may experience it as a rejection of himself rather than as anxiety related to the pregnancy. A woman who makes love without experiencing pleasure is setting up unfortunate barriers between herself and her husband. If she does not speak of her feelings, he may not speak of his—but he is more likely to go to someone else for love and warmth. A man who feels he is loved will be much more able to pass through a period of sexual abstention without feeling pushed out.

• **"We abstained during the period 8 to 13 weeks, on the advice of the obstetrician—there was the threat of a miscarriage. We both felt positive about that. We thought it was helping to keep the baby, and we were willing to do anything to do that."**

Most women who report this fear of miscarriage report a concomitant decrease in their sexual desire. Because they and their husbands are concerned for the health and safety of the fetus, they do not seem to experience as much frustration from the period of abstinence as they might under other circumstances.

Some use restraint instead of total abstinence:

• **"Following intercourse early in my pregnancy (before confirmation, actually), I had**

24

some vaginal bleeding. We had been using the female superior position, but this incident frightened us, so we abandoned this position for the remainder of my pregnancy. We figured it caused too deep penetration and that his penis thrust too hard against my cervix. Also, I had usually been having three or more orgasms during intercourse, but uterine contractions following orgasm had me concerned that some damage might be done to the baby, so I held myself down to one or two orgasms. Despite these accommodations to my 'condition,' lovemaking was as delightful as it had ever been. I felt wonderfully healthy during my entire pregnancy and desired my husband as much as I always had. We had intercourse as frequently as before—about three times a week—and continued to do so until about three days before our son was born."

Whether the fear of a miscarriage is well founded or whether it is unfounded, if a woman is very anxious that intercourse or orgasm may cause a miscarriage early in pregnancy, she may enjoy giving sexual pleasure to her husband through genital manipulation and a general massage without receiving any direct stimulation herself.

For all of the couples quoted so far, the fear of miscarriage was confirmed by a physician. Modifications of sexual behavior were seen as therapeutic measures. In some cases, however, fears are left over from unspecific rumors or simply from misinformation. They can have a sad effect on the couple's lovemaking during pregnancy.

• "I went through many stages in my attitude toward sex during my pregnancy. At the onset, I was hesitant to have sex basically because I had the fear that something was going to happen to the baby. My husband tried to explain to me that this was nonsense, and every time we had sex I did not at all enjoy it. I was very frightened instead. I then tried to read up on the subject. After reading, speaking to my doctor, and getting reassurance from my husband, I realized that sex wouldn't affect my baby. It took me a while, but after a month or so, my desire for sex increased and my fear disappeared. I really think that this topic should be discussed between patient and doctor at the first visit—especially in the case of a first pregnancy—so that the fears such as mine could be lessened at the very beginning."

At such an anxious period, a couple might do well to relax by massaging and caressing each other and talking over their fears rather than by proceeding unwillingly with other sexual behavior. True lovemaking means staying in touch emotionally as well as physically. If one partner makes love just to please the other and in spite of his or her own deepest feelings, he or she will build up hostility and resentment instead of warmth and pleasure.

• "When we first made our announcement to relatives and friends, I remember hearing that we should avoid intercourse on the days I would have had my period. It sounded farfetched at the time, and soon afterwards, while browsing through a book on pregnancy, I read that this was only an old wives' tale. I decided then that any restriction would only be accepted from the OB."

- "I remember hearing that orgasm would deprive the fetus of oxygen and/or cause miscarriage. Then my mother said that her doctor had told her while pregnant with me that she should not have relations after the seventh month 'to prevent dirt from getting into the uterus.' I figure these are just old wives' tales."

The rumor that orgasm may deprive the fetus of oxygen is based on the observable fact that there is a slight change in the fetal heart rate during orgasms. This is so small a change, however, that most scientific investigators have maintained that it has no adverse affect on the fetus.

Vaginal infections are nothing to be more afraid of in pregnancy than at other times. The fetus is safely protected from any "dirt" that might be introduced into the vagina. He is inside an unbroken sac of fluid, and that sac is safely protected within the uterus which is sealed off from the vagina by the cervix. One can't help but wonder what was meant by "dirt"; if there is a question of the man's hygiene, it should be dealt with whether his wife is pregnant or not.

If a woman does pick up some kind of infection, such as monilia, it can make sexual intercourse painful (pregnant or nonpregnant). Fortunately, medical science has come up with effective cures. If a woman has to abstain from intercourse during treatment, she can still participate in many satisfying forms of lovemaking and enjoy orgasms achieved through oral sex or manual stimulation without the penis entering the vagina.

28

There is one other rare complication of pregnancy that is sometimes misunderstood:

- **"Having heard that cunnilingus during pregnancy was dangerous (something about introducing air into the uterus) we abandoned this practice."**

It is true that air should not be forced into the vagina during pregnancy or any other time. This is one of the few hazards of sex, a rare phenomena called air embolism.[4] It is rare because not many people blow into the vagina with sufficient force to cause air to pass into the uterus and from there into the woman's bloodstream. Nevertheless, couples who enjoy oral sex should be aware of this one restriction. It should not cause them to stop enjoying cunnilingus. However, some men want to stop having oral sex with their wives for other reasons. They are not always able to realize quite what is different. Perhaps it is the proximity of the fetus, but more likely it's the extra discharge and change in smell and/or taste of the vagina that is typical in pregnancy. The discharge is a result of the extra lubrication created by the increased blood supply to the genitals during pregnancy. Douching will not make it stop and is of no particular benefit during pregnancy or any other time.

- **"The only thing I really missed when I was pregnant was oral sex. My husband absolutely refuses to perform cunnilingus when I'm pregnant. Even he is not sure why.'**

A man who does not care for the odors that may accompany pregnancy or sexual arousal, may

enjoy massaging his wife with scented oil that changes her odor or her taste.

For many, many couples, lovemaking is not much different during the first trimester of pregnancy than at other times:

• **"It has been pretty much 'sex as usual.' There are periods of greater concentration of desire and periods of lessened desire, but this has been true of our sex life during all the times we've known each other, and as far as I can tell, pregnancy has not established a distinct new pattern."**

• **"As far as sexual desire during pregnancy goes, I'd say that the first three months was normal. (We have been together for eight years and we have sex on the average of three times a week, but often going through phases of more or less.) Because my body didn't look pregnant, I didn't really feel pregnant. (I had no morning sickness or problems.)"**

• **"During the first five or six months all was as usual, except that I was occasionally more tired than normal. There was no feeling of anxiety or fear on my part or my husband's. Sex was satisfying and frequent."**

• **"The only thing that affected my sex drive during pregnancy was the tired feeling I had most of the time—especially during my second pregnancy, since I couldn't nap when I needed it because I had a toddler running around the house. I continued to enjoy sex throughout but had to change to the side or reverse position** (which we enjoyed very much) as my belly grew. My husband's sex drive was unchanged."

• "The delight of our lovemaking did not diminish during pregnancy. There was a little more carefulness, a little less abandonment, and a resultant reduction in spontaneity. These did not affect the joy. For instance, shortly after we knew definitely of the pregnancy, we discontinued use of the pillow under the hips. It made a minor difference, but only for a time or two. Then it was as though we never had used the pillow, in terms of pleasure. If I pounded less or became more gentle than usual, the thrill of having a special reason to be protective of both my wife and the baby compensated completely for any largely unconscious holding back in the satisfaction of my hungers."

• "Upon deciding that I should become pregnant, the continuation of our good sex life was prominent in my mind. My husband's attitude was that people who are open with each other and responsive to each other's needs sexually under ordinary conditions would maintain this relationship during the pregnancy. I was not convinced of this based on what I had heard from others; however, I accepted it and got pregnant.

"By the way, 'what I had heard from others' was not to be believed. One close friend confided that she had told her husband that her doctor told her 'no sex' for the duration of pregnancy, as she had trouble conceiving. She felt it was just too bad for her husband. She told me I probably wouldn't be able to get away with ab-

33

staining for nine months, but certainly by the end of the seventh I ought to stop. Other time limits varied, but the general consensus was six weeks before the due date you locked up your gates and your husband goes berserk. To all of these kinds of warnings I wanted to ask, 'What about me? Who do I do for six weeks?' I asked once, and the reply was 'Don't worry. You won't feel like it.'

"I have to admit that during the first three months of nausea there were times I didn't feel like it. For the most part, however, our sex life was as active as it always was. Once I stopped feeling sick, my desire definitely increased so much that I masturbated many times. (Before my pregnancy I masturbated occasionally.)"

Another woman remarks on the same cultural attitude that women are not supposed to enjoy sexual relations and may be able to use pregnancy as an excuse to avoid them:

• "I feel that pregnancy can and is used as an excuse to lessen sexual relations. It's true that in the last month or so not only is position a problem, but psychologically I felt worn and uncomfortable due to back and abdominal pressures. But sexual experiences were enjoyable during my pregnancies."

In fact, many, many women and men enjoy sex during pregnancy!

• "Sexual excitation was particularly intense during both the first and last trimesters."

34

- "During the first two or three months my wife was particularly affectionate, which made me enjoy sex more than ever."

The increased pleasure in sex after conception seems to be related to more than simply the freedom from contraception:

- "I was very turned on during my pregnancy, always feeling sexy. My nausea and headaches didn't interfere with sex. I guess it's really the only time (until menopause) when the two of you don't have to worry about protecting yourselves. It's like that on the Pill, too, but this is even better. My husband and I really enjoyed knowing that I was pregnant and there was a little person inside me, oblivious to the fact that we were making love. Like a harmless little voyeur. It became a game because there was actually a third party in bed with us. So we had a lot of sex then and it was very carefree and good."

- "I was feeling, before the pregnancy, quite sexy (for me), aware of my body, enjoying appreciative comments. This is not my most usual state. After I became pregnant, for a number of months I felt almost like a sex maniac. I was relieved to hear that for many women the sex drive either increases or decreases during pregnancy for many reasons. For me, I think the sense of freedom and of spontaneity because I did not have to put in the darned diaphragm played a role. Also, the feelings I had to start with about my body were heightened by a sense

I.F.P.

of pride and excitement. I felt positively glow-ing. Back to sex—I think I could have had inter-course nightly, or almost. We continued our usual pattern of two or three times a week; more at times, sometimes not at all for a short period of stress. I communicated my drives to my husband verbally, but our busy schedule and—I guess—his drives, meant that our sex life remained as it had been. I don't know if I was exactly frustrated, but sex was certainly on my mind. I don't think either that a need to be reassured of my attractiveness, being loved, was behind this particular drive, though this is usually an element for me. At this time I felt no sense of insecurity."

This woman is not alone in feeling a surge of sexual desire early in pregnancy. Women with usually low level drives sometimes feel a new urge. Couples may have to talk about their changing feelings.

• "Well, for starters, I've always had trouble having sex. It seems to hurt me, and if I have it one night, I can't have it again for two days. I feel my self-consciousness about my weight, etc., inhibits me from really being able to relax or try anything but the usual position of man on top. My feelings about myself changed when I first became pregnant. I seemed more eager to have sex, and I wanted it much more often."

• "During my first stage of pregnancy (two to four months) I found sex enjoyable. The first climax I ever reached was during this time."

• "In the early months, pregnancy added a new dimension to our sexual relationship: our child was growing within me; yet nothing was different externally. We took great delight in sharing this important facet of our lives, knowing what had grown from such a pleasurable experience. We also felt quite pleased with ourselves . . . we had become pregnant immediately after deciding that we wanted to start our family."

• "If anything, I became more interested in my body's reaction to sex—probably a psychological intensification connected with profound emotion, fertility, and procreation."

• "To begin with, I'm on a super high when I am pregnant, and both times I felt as if I were the most special human being in the world. The indirect result of the euphoric feelings that I experienced were related to the pleasures I had during sex. Our sexual relations have always been good, and for the first trimester of my pregnancies I became insatiable, probably feeling most feminine and desirable and special."

• "In the first trimester, I felt very pretty, feminine and sexy, in spite of the nausea and persistent vomiting. Sex was very enjoyable, contraception was to be forgotten and now it just was a worry-less type of relationship."

For some, the increased pleasure in lovemaking is quite specifically focused:

• "During the first and second trimesters we had a wonderful time with my new oversized

38

breasts. I've always wanted larger breasts and lo and behold there they were. At first we couldn't touch them because they were sore, but once the soreness left, we were off."

The engorgement of breast tissue that occurs with pregnancy does cause nipple tenderness in the early months of the first pregnancy, especially during lovemaking, for sexual arousal causes yet more blood to come to the already engorged areas. The tenderness passes as the body accommodates to the new conditions.

- "I felt more womanly and even voluptuous, the latter feeling based on the fact that my breasts increased several bra sizes. Both my husband and I got a kick out of that."

- "I have always had small breasts, and it seems that the only time I have a halfway substantial bosom is when I'm pregnant. It is probably mainly psychological, but I have always found just the idea of having larger breasts very exciting. So when I'm pregnant, I'm in my glory. Also I have found that the supersensitivity of my breasts during the early months makes me become aroused much easier and faster during foreplay. My husband also seems to enjoy this aspect of my being pregnant.
  "I know that during pregnancy there is an increased blood supply to the genital area, and I've always felt as though all my wires were exposed, so to speak. When my husband made love to me I was able to reach a climax faster, again because of my supersensitivity."

Patterns of making love do not have to change very radically during the first trimester because there is no pronounced change in body shape. However, many of the people quoted in this chapter testify to the fact that sexual behavior is influenced by pregnancy even before the condition is observable from the outside. Some couples find greater joy together simply because of pregnancy; others in the same situation become anxious and uncomfortable. Some lose all interest in sex because of fatigue and nausea; some experience the symptoms but ignore them and enjoy sex; others never experience these symptoms.

The basic physiological changes are fairly predictable, but the individual reactions to these changes depend on many, many factors which reflect the individual personality of the man and woman and the relationship between them. One woman remarked:

• **"I think how you feel about sex during pregnancy depends to a great extent on how you felt about sex before you became pregnant and also how you and your husband feel about the pregnancy itself. If the pregnancy was unwelcome by either or both parties, then there is already tension, and that doesn't contribute to a very worthwhile relationship—sexual or otherwise."**

Of course, attitudes toward sex and attitudes toward the pregnancy are among the factors which influence the feelings about lovemaking during pregnancy. But there are other factors as well. Pregnancy is an important but mysterious time. It has always been particularly laden with taboos and arcane ceremonies. It is an extraordinarily personal event that takes place deep within a woman's body; yet it belongs to the entire race, for it is critical to the survival of our kind. Similarly, sexual behavior is private, but its consequences affect society at large.

Both pregnancy and sexuality have long been taboo subjects. Even the medical profession has been hesitant to explore them. We are only beginning to learn how normal, healthy couples respond in their personal lives to this big event. As the taboos fall away, we are starting to see that many traditional fears have been ungrounded. Pregnancy, like sexuality, can become a part of life filled with great satisfaction and joy.

A tender pat and an erotic caress reflect very different moods, but they both convey the same message: "I love you." It is a message that both men and women need to hear throughout pregnancy almost more than at other times in their lives, because the strangeness of the woman's changing body may make it hard for her to accept her image and feel confident about her ability to attract her partner. Her need for reassurance and affection is vastly increased. At the same time, the man has to feel that his partner's love and attention is not entirely concentrated on the growing child—which is to say, inwardly. He needs to feel that some of it is still directed toward him.

Making love is always more than sexual intercourse. During pregnancy, it is all the intimate moments between father and mother which nurtures them in their adjustment to parenthood. The ongoing expressions of affection keep alive the role of lovers for a young couple confronting the strange new role of parents. Making love, giving and receiving signs of caring, of tenderness, and of passion, keeps the couple in touch with each other and keeps them sensitive to their own and the other's physical and emotional needs.

● "We've had a wonderful, passionate love life, and to now create a little person from our love just goes beyond words. It has added a whole new dimension to our lives and feelings toward one another. I feel we've grown as people, friends, and lovers. I'll never forget that night when my husband looked at me with warm, loving eyes and said, 'You want to make a baby?' He was so cute. I guess I did, because all of a sudden we made a baby."

The Second Trimester

There are many different patterns of interest in sexual behavior and desire during pregnancy. Most of the replies we received to our questionnaire reported a continuing increase in desire through the first two trimesters, dropping off as the third trimester progressed. Although this was the most common pattern in our sample, a large percentage of men and women felt that there was no significant change in their sexual desire or frequency during pregnancy, and a few reported a series of ups and downs throughout the pregnancy.

Masters and Johnson observed a small number of women under laboratory conditions and received written answers to questionnaires from a larger number of men and women. They discovered a general pattern of a decrease of interest in the first trimester, an increase in the second trimester to a level higher than before pregnancy, and a dropping off as the third trimester progressed.[5] Some of our respondents reflected this pattern.

Similarly, James A. Kenny reported that in 33 women who responded to a questionnaire, there was a general pattern of no change in the first trimester, a slight increase in the second trimester, and a decrease in desire, frequency, and enjoyment in the third (although apparently the number of orgasms experienced by the women remained the same).[6]

In a report on 19 women, Celia J. Falicov reported that pregnancy had a generalized adverse effect on sexual adjustment.[7] She noted a decline during the first trimester and a relative increase during the second trimester and the early weeks of the third trimester before dropping off again at the end of pregnancy. Her pattern is similar to that of Masters and Johnson and Kenny, except that the middle trimester does not go above prepregnancy levels.

In several studies made in the United States and Europe, doctors report that sexual behavior diminished progressively as pregnancy proceeded.[8] Solberg, Butler, and Wagner found similar results in 260 women in the Seattle area.[9] "For most women, coital activity declines in a linear fashion once pregnancy is discovered." We also had some respondents who described this decline. One put it succinctly! "My interest in sex was: first trimester, very much; second trimester, so-so; and third trimester, not at all."

Solberg, Butler, and Wagner found some women who responded like the majority of ours; they say that "despite the significant and steady reduction in sexual behavior for most women, some increased their activity."

Our study, like Masters and Johnson's and Kenny's, shows many women who have levels of sexual behavior and interest that are greater than before pregnancy. It should be remembered that our reports, like those of Masters and Johnson, came from volunteers, from people who were open enough about intimate sexual matters to want to write about them. Additionally, our population, like Kenny's, had access to childbirth preparation or human sexuality education and might therefore be presumed to have had more help dealing with their problems as they arose. Solberg, Butler, and Wagner point out that only 5 women of their 260 were told by physicians about sexual practices that might be used if coitus was no longer comfortable and only 10 percent were given recommendations about alternative positions to try. Perhaps the ups in sexual coitus that often seem to follow the downs in our reports can sometimes be attributed to professional intervention in the form of education and reassurance.

The majority of people in all studies report a gradual decrease either in interest or (more frequently) in activity, as the last trimester progresses. As one of our women put it: "Toward the end of my pregnancy my desires lessened, not because of any physical discomfort during intercourse, but because I became terribly uncomfortable all over."

But a very real minority continues to enjoy sexual relations to the very end: "I was more interested in sex during my pregnancy than ever before, and increasingly so as pregnancy progressed."

There are so many factors influencing the ups and downs of sexual interest and lovemaking during the course of pregnancy that general patterns that result from statistical studies are often irrelevant to the experience of one particular couple. A woman who has a general trend toward increased interest in lovemaking may have a few weeks of disinterest along the way. An individual whose interest had been on a long, steady decline can sud-

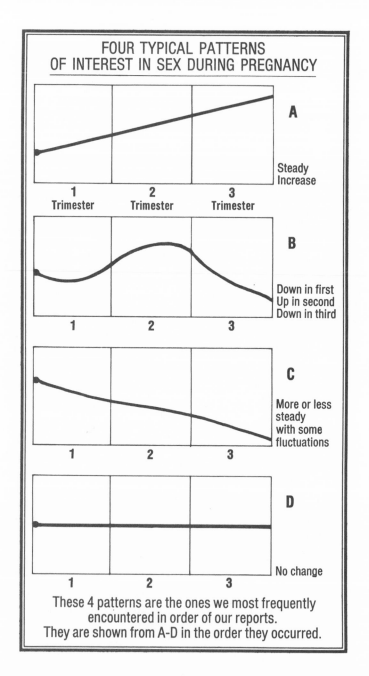

FOUR TYPICAL PATTERNS
OF INTEREST IN SEX DURING PREGNANCY

A
Steady
Increase

| 1 | 2 | 3 |
| Trimester | Trimester | Trimester |

B
Down in first
Up in second
Down in third

| 1 | 2 | 3 |

C
More or less
steady
with some
fluctuations

| 1 | 2 | 3 |

D
No change

| 1 | 2 | 3 |

These 4 patterns are the ones we most frequently
encountered in order of our reports.
They are shown from A-D in the order they occurred.

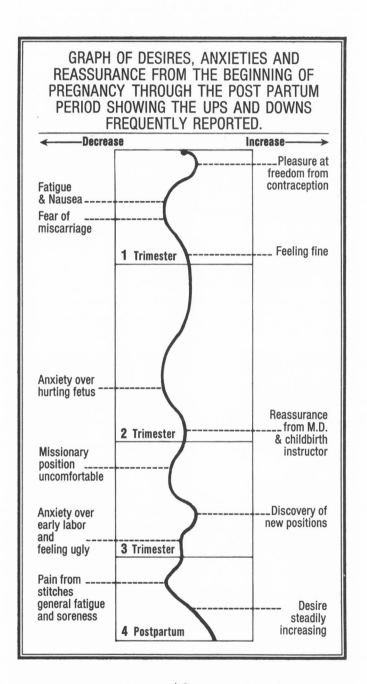

GRAPH OF DESIRES, ANXIETIES AND REASSURANCE FROM THE BEGINNING OF PREGNANCY THROUGH THE POST PARTUM PERIOD SHOWING THE UPS AND DOWNS FREQUENTLY REPORTED.

←—Decrease   Increase—→

Pleasure at freedom from contraception

Fatigue & Nausea

Fear of miscarriage

1 Trimester   Feeling fine

Anxiety over hurting fetus

Reassurance from M.D. & childbirth instructor

2 Trimester

Missionary position uncomfortable

Anxiety over early labor and feeling ugly   Discovery of new positions

3 Trimester

Pain from stitches general fatigue and soreness

Desire steadily increasing

4 Postpartum

49

denly reach a new phase and have a renewed desire to make love with her partner. There is a great deal going on during pregnancy, and most of it affects the relationship between the mother and father to be. This relationship inevitably affects feelings about lovemaking. And so we turn, not to the statistics, but to the actual accounts of real people describing their ups and downs as they deal with issues of sexuality and loving during their pregnancies.

Whichever pattern holds, the second trimester is generally the most comfortable period of pregnancy for making love. The initial adjustment to the idea of pregnancy has generally been made; if there were bouts of nausea or fatigue, they have generally passed. The chance of miscarriage is virtually gone. The abdomen may be starting to bulge, but it is generally not yet large enough to present much of an obstacle to lovemaking.

● **"In all three pregnancies, we enjoyed sex more during the middle trimester, by which time I was less tired, less nauseous, and less worried about miscarriage."**

There are very few rational complaints at this time. However, there are some, and they shall be dealt with before turning to the longer list of exciting surprises that are apt to occur during the second trimester.

Unfortunately, body chemistry does not read books and has never heard of the trimester system. Morning sickness does not magically disappear on a certain day of the month. Some women are plagued by nausea and vomiting throughout their pregnancies!

50

• "Since the first two months of pregnancy, I have felt seasick most of the time. Whether because of that or for some other unknown reason my interest in sex (though not in affection) has lapsed."

The fatigue frequently found in early pregnancy still may occur:

• "Due to early discomforts, severe pains in my sides, and shortness of breath during sexual intercourse at approximately twenty-six weeks of pregnancy sexual intercourse was not enjoyable and we were advised to stop. My desire had not increased or decreased, but I was disappointed more for my husband's sake when we had to stop so early."

Fears—particularly of miscarriage—may also persist:

• "The frequency of sexual intercourse decreased from the first trimester. Although we were aware that there was no good reason to decrease intercourse, we did so anyway. This was my second pregnancy. The first ended in miscarriage soon after intercourse. As a result we were afraid even though we were told and read that intercourse had little if any influence on the course of pregnancy."

Quite a few women simply report that their desire dropped off in the second trimester:

• "During the second trimester, I found sex to be boring, dull, and a waste of time. Being

51

temperamental during this time I enjoyed oral sex better than a normal man-and-woman relationship."

This particular woman had experienced her first orgasm during the first trimester and enjoyed lovemaking more than at any other time in her life. Once she felt the baby move, however, she did not feel it was appropriate to have anyone else "inside" her. Therefore she no longer enjoyed vaginal penetration.

Another had trouble with vaginal discomfort.

• **"Toward the end of my fourth month, I began to experience discomfort and pain whenever my husband entered me. Why I don't know. I just know that it hurt. So we decided to abstain from sex until after the baby was born. As for my sexual desires, they were still there and as strong as ever. So my husband and I indulged in masturbation and oral sex, something we had enjoyed before. We missed the actual lovemaking, but we knew that sooner or later we would be able to indulge again. Within four weeks of giving birth, we were back to having intercourse as often as we had before I became pregnant. No more discomfort or pain, just love."**

Many women experience **less** discomfort when their husbands enter them because of the extra lubrication that comes along with the genital engorgement of pregnancy. But one woman was **so** engorged that there was not as much room for her husband's penis:

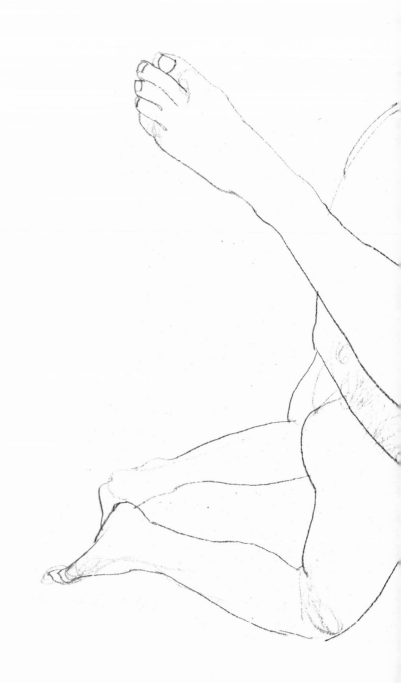

• "My genitals were so swollen there was hardly room for my husband's penis. The sides of my vagina touched, even when I was excited. It wasn't like this with my first and second pregnancies."

Both couples coped effectively with the changes by relying on alternative forms of love-making instead of coitus.

Husbands begin to get more involved in the pregnancy during this trimester. They begin to see the abdomen changing shape and growing. Even more importantly, they may be able to feel the fetus move. This makes it more real for them.

• "The second three months our sex life continued along as usual; even though the fetus was very active I knew that we couldn't do anything to hurt it. When we made love I didn't—and still don't—really think about the baby at all. My husband expressed a bit of trepidation from time to time, but since I experienced no discomfort, his fears were alleviated."

Other husbands have more trouble being comfortable with the changes:

• "After the first three months, my husband said that intercourse was uncomfortable for him in any of our varied positions. As a result, I was very frustrated, which I attempted to relieve with masturbation. Having, however, heard one old wives' tale about danger to the fetus from orgasm, I was apprehensive about it."

● "My husband and I had relations up until my fourth month. After that time my husband had anxieties saying he could not bring himself to have sex with my stomach protruding. (He was really afraid of hurting me or the baby—no matter what I said.) This was really hard since my sexual desire increased greatly as the pregnancy progressed."

This couple did not ask for help. One can only feel infinitely sad that they did not visit the doctor together to discuss their problem with him. It's not always easy for the physician to guess the trouble some of his patients may have. But it is brought home to us how much couples as well as professionals have to learn to communicate with each other on these important matters.

A husband tried to understand his problem:

● "I think that men must learn somehow to know what physical and emotional changes will take place in his wife, and enjoy them. I couldn't. Perhaps, also, jealousy in not being able to participate is a factor. This is the one thing no man can do."

Another father was very aware of his jealousy. He was asked during the first class he attended for childbirth education why he wanted to participate with his partner. He answered, "I'm really jealous. I wish I could have a big belly from time to time and experience what it feels like to have a baby inside me." He enjoyed his wife's new shape, wistfully wishing his body could change like hers.

57

A woman who wrote that sex decreased in the second trimester and became nonexistent in the third gave her explanations:

- **"I was very pregnant from my fourth month on, and I was afraid of the man-on-top position in spite of the fact that I take pride in being an extremely well-informed patient and knew very well that no harm could come to the baby.**

  "At certain times, probably due to emotional highs and lows of pregnancy, I would feel that the only reason my husband wanted me was to let me know that he cared when I couldn't imagine how I could be sexually attractive with such a huge abdomen."

Those emotional highs and lows play a part in the experience of making love throughout pregnancy, but they seem to be mentioned most frequently in the middle. Symptomatically, this is the "quiet time." There is not much going on— pregnancy has been confirmed, but labor and delivery are still many months away. And yet for the couple, this is the period of the great discovery, for it is during the middle trimester that the baby's movements can be felt for the first time. For this or other reasons, there is often a period of turning inward, for discovering one's deepest feelings about the meaning of the pregnancy and about the act of becoming a parent. It is also the time when the couple must begin to contend with the reality of the changing body as more than just enlarged breasts, freedom from contraception, and occasional fatigue or nausea. As pregnancy gradually begins to include a kicking fetus and a large abdo-

59

men, husband and wife must begin to make adjustments.

- "I found our times of making love became shorter in duration and frequency. As the pressure of my husband on top of me became uncomfortable (about the fourth month), I told him I didn't mind not having an orgasm and that I preferred his coming quickly. Prior to my becoming pregnant I was much more willing to experiment with different positions, but I wasn't feeling free enough during this stage of my pregnancy to be athletic. I think this stage was the most difficult for me. I was emotionally more vulnerable than usual, and I hadn't fully accepted the changes that were going on inside of me. I still enjoyed oral sex and resented my husband when he said he didn't want to participate in oral sex due to the increased amount and strength of vaginal discharge.

"After the fifth month, we began to discover new positions that were comfortable (such as his lying on top but partly sideways so that most of his weight was off me), and since then I have been enjoying sex more. I think a large part of this is because I finally believed that I was not going to lose the baby and therefore I felt much freer physically. My husband's fears were just as strong as mine, and now he too has relaxed. I think the fear of losing the baby, plus my feeling in the early part of mid-pregnancy that my body was less attractive (this was pushed by my husband's change in acceptance of me as I saw it—i.e., the cessation of oral sex) were the two major reasons why I found sex less enjoyable for a while."

60

There are other new sensations to get used to:

- "One time I had an orgasm during my fifth or sixth month, which caused my belly to contract in one spasm. I was scared I was hurting the baby or doing something wrong. I spoke to my doctor and he said this was quite common, though it didn't always happen. I spoke to friends and they said they had never heard of such a thing. Then I took preparation classes and learned that orgasms would not hurt anything, so I relaxed and enjoyed them again (though I still have a little fear).

  "One of the most exciting times was when I felt life for the first time. I was all alone sitting up in bed reading when all of a sudden a huge grin spread from one ear to the other. I began to giggle and talk to myself. I couldn't wait till my husband got home. Of course I made him put his hand on my belly to feel the flutter. Well, fifteen minutes later, a very patient man said, 'Maybe another time; he's probably asleep.'"

Many women who are afraid of becoming unattractive to their husbands are pleasantly surprised to learn how very involved the men feel in the pregnancy.

- "As my body changed in shape, I feared I'd be less attractive to my husband, but this proved to be quite false, both of us taking great pleasure in my new shape. I became very conscious of my shape and loved it, and my husband found this very arousing. He would caress my belly as if it were a new erogenous zone."

• "In the middle months, I became anxious to share sex often before I 'lost control' of my body. I was sure that I wouldn't feel sexual during the heavy months; that I wouldn't be appealing to my husband; and that we would be told to abstain which would create tension for both of us. My projections were inaccurate, and reality was much more pleasant than I had imagined."

Nevertheless, the changing body is a very real issue in the husband-wife relationship.

• "As the pregnancy became more and more evident, my body image began to suffer. Having been chubby as a preteen and teen-ager, I could not separate my feelings of again having an undesirable body from this natural and necessary stage. However, I found that my husband was responding very positively toward my body. The idea of my carrying his baby seemed sexually exciting to him. I also found that close friends—two in particular—were also admittedly turned on by me. I was surprised and greatly appreciated the attention, considering I was feeling so awkward looking. On the other hand, it's amusing to note that construction workers stopped making sounds and comments when I passed them on the street.

"Because I began to feel during the second trimester and into the third that my body was not really attractive, I began to make a special effort to please my husband sexually. We had in our marriage a fairly open and active sexual relationship and so although nothing we were doing was new, the frequency of these other

65

positions, etc., was greater. Oral sex, anal stimulation, mutual masturbation now played a greater role in our lovemaking. I had nowhere heard that orgasms were dangerous during pregnancy, and I continued to enjoy them during sex."

For many, many women, sexual desire reaches a new plateau during the middle of pregnancy. The descriptions are sometimes so dramatic that it is hard to ignore the possibility that there are physiological factors at work. In fact, the hormonal changes of pregnancy are essentially the same as the changes of sexual arousal. Engorgement of breast and genital tissue with extra blood, lubrication of the vagina, increased steroid and estrogen production—these are symptoms associated with sexual arousal, yet they have become a part of the pregnant woman's basic body state. When she becomes sexually aroused, she experiences yet further increases in all these things.

Because of the nature of some of the changes of pregnancy, it is not surprising that a certain number of women respond to their pregnant bodies with a subjective experience of increased sexual desire.

• **"Sex during my pregnancy seemed to continue 'as usual' in frequency and pleasure for the first several months, then suddenly increased in the last half. My interest was particularly greater. I felt good having intercourse, which reinforced assurances given me by my OB that sexual life should continue as previous to pregnancy. Intellectually I wondered at first if intercourse could cause me to lose the fetus, but**

68

these fears seemed fleeting because I felt good, and everything I read led me to believe it was safe."

• "I enjoyed sex in the middle of pregnancy more than at any other time in our marriage."

• "Sexual desire has increased steadily after those first few months. Positions have not been difficult to find."

• "Sex is most enjoyable in the second trimester of pregnancy because you're past the morning sickness and before the leg cramps and hugeness. Desire for sex increased during the second trimester—was decreased the first three months but not as much during the last three. Only problem I felt was the need for frequent washings because of extra vaginal discharge at that time."

• "Sexually, the second trimester was the best for me. My desire increased past pre-pregnancy levels. It became easier for me to become lubricated, although I don't know if this was psychological or physiological. Among the changes I noticed in my body during the second trimester was that my genitals seemed enlarged most of the time. I had never read anywhere that this would occur, and at this writing I only assume that others experience it too."

• "I found that during the second trimester I would feel occasional surges of sexual arousal that were not associated with physical contact at all—almost as if it were a physiological rather than an emotional triggering mechanism. These would last only a short time and might occur during the work day as well as at home. We had intercourse somewhat less during the second trimester and essentially not at all by the end of the last trimester. We discussed why and concluded that it was becoming physically too cumbersome and that we weren't really that anxious to experiment with new approaches—it became not worth all the effort involved and we seemed content to be emotionally close and do more 'hugging and kissing' than actual intercourse."

• "Now in my second trimester, I'm back to my old self plus a little more. Several times I've awakened in the middle of the night with fantastic vaginal sensations. I don't know if there's a female counterpart to the male 'wet dream,' but I don't remember dreaming and I've never had this happen in the past."

• "I found my sexual desires heightened after my fourth month of pregnancy and continued until the end of my eighth month. My orgasms were stronger and longer than usual. My husband was not always available when I desired him. I found myself indulging in and enjoying masturbation more than I care to admit."

• "I may have masturbated a few times or tried and given it up because it didn't fulfill any need—my memory is somewhat hazy. But I did want sex more in the middle of pregnancy."

The last two women quoted reveal some guilt around their increased erotic needs and their use of masturbation as a solution. Masturbation is an activity that often evokes feelings of guilt and may be particularly disturbing during pregnancy. Wagner and Solberg report that "the majority (50 to 60 percent) of those who previously masturbated abstained from the practice during the nine-month period."[10] This is in keeping with their finding that most of the women in their study had fewer orgasms and made love less often as pregnancy progressed. Falicov suggests that such women are afraid to "let go" sexually during pregnancy. "The specific focus of this fear (often described as a 'holding back') seems to be the avoidance of the experience of orgasm, which tended to invoke an image of releasing the fetus." [11] Reassurance that as far as we know orgasm will not harm the baby seems to alleviate the fear of masturbation as it alleviates the fear of intercourse (see discussion of orgasm on page 12).

Those women who do feel a heightened desire and an increased intensity of erotic feelings may find that they enjoy masturbation during pregnancy even when they do not masturbate at other times in their lives. Others, particularly single women, may find themselves masturbating more than usual. As with orgasm achieved by other means, women who have spotting, pain, or reasons to suspect they might miscarry, may need to abstain from masturbating to orgasm. It would be a good idea for the woman to consult her doctor whether or not orgasm should be avoided in her case.

Talking about her increased sexual drive, one woman said:

• "My husband has handled these and other changes in me with great ability. He caters to my emotional ups and downs as if it were his only concern. Although he isn't having the hormonal changes I am, this is a very new and emotional experience for him, too, and I'm trying not to act too irrational in front of him. An example of how I confuse him might be the way I reacted to the change in my body shape. At the beginning, I 'felt fat,' and getting dressed to go out was a trying experience. Now, I drag him on long walks so I can show off the two most important people in my life—my husband and the baby we made in my blossoming belly. I don't think of my body as being visible proof of our sex life, but of the incredible blessing and miracle we're sharing."

Making love in pregnancy is fraught with joys and problems. Like making love at any other time, it is influenced by how the couple feels about themselves and about each other. One father wrote:

• "In thinking about all of this it occurs to me that the bulk of sexual problems during and just after pregnancy must really stem from the problems that exist, perhaps on a lower level, in the relationship before pregnancy. If there is an open and ongoing relationship and understanding of physical and emotional changes, and a genuine sympathy with the other person's feelings to begin with, a lot of trouble can be averted. If the sexual relationship is based upon the reality of giving and receiving pleasure, rather than a commercial sexual imagery, so much misunderstanding could be avoided. It

could be so nice if people could learn quickly to be at the stage of enjoying each other's bodies, rather than admiring them, and opening their minds to each other's pleasure rather than closing their minds into the process of maneuvering pleasure out of the other person for themselves."

But the changes of pregnancy add new moods and new responses to an already complex system. Life may seem more unpredictable as the changes keep right on occurring, for pregnancy is progressive. Conception starts a chain of events that keep on going until the end. The second trimester is the midway point, but it is not a stable condition. It inevitably gives way to the third trimester—a period during which every woman knows—undeniably—that she is "really" pregnant.

The Third Trimester

The most conspicuous feature of the last three months of pregnancy is the big belly. Simple things like shifting one's body from the back to the side to a sitting position, lifting one's legs, or getting out of bed may become awkward and difficult. The purely physical movements of lovemaking may become too tiring to be enjoyable. One woman who was not interested in lovemaking in her ninth month remarked:

- **"I have such difficulty turning over in bed by now, I'm content to get into my 'sleeping position' and stay there."**

Motions which have always been a graceful or routine reflex, such as bending forward or arching back, may become conscious and performed with difficulty:

- **"It is difficult to find a comfortable position in bed, and moving around actively during lovemaking is rather a problem. I think I'm so tired at night not only because of the pregnancy but also because of active days of shopping, visiting, and 'getting things in' before the baby arrives."**

75

- "After the seventh month, my husband felt that having sex required too much in the way of gymnastics, and we had no sex from then to the end."

- "We enjoyed sex during pregnancy on a regular basis, although not as much as when I wasn't pregnant. We enjoyed it less as the pregnancy advanced simply because it was more uncomfortable. There was no change in desire."

- "Sometimes it was tricky, but because of mutual desire, we managed. My husband's good Marine Corps background and his calisthenics came in handy and usually left him winded and us laughing."

Formerly quick reactions may change to slow motion, conscious effort and require a new approach. Here are remarks from several men and women who have adapted the lovemaking to the new circumstances:

- "On the occasions when we might formerly have thrown ourselves upon each other with wild abandon, we are now more apt to snuggle circumspectly."

- "During the last trimester I developed a larger belly, so I spent most of the time on top of my husband because it was easier; or else he would enter from behind. I started to tire faster, thus not lasting too long in our lovemaking. Then it was too uncomfortable on top, and in the last month my husband felt a little nervous entering me. It didn't bother me at all. We

78

satisfied each other orally or manually. We did say to each other at one time we couldn't wait to get back to normal because we have a very satisfying, fun sex life."

• "My husband and I tried a new posture, with me bending over the bathroom sink for rear entry. I found that to be very enjoyable."

• "Basically, we've been able to remain fairly versatile. The only positions we've avoided during this last month are those which provide maximum penetration since they cause a feeling of pressure which makes us slightly apprehensive. We've always engaged in oral-genital sex and I guess that's what we'll do for the first month after the baby comes. Many women have told me that I'll be really turned off sex that first month or so, but it's hard to believe from the way I feel now. Back to positions, I guess the one most used (by us) are the woman-on-top, front-to-back side position, front-to-front side position, and missionary—or variations of it."

• "After the increased size of my abdomen made finding a comfortable position difficult, we usually used the female-dominant position or occasionally rear entry. This cut down on the frequency of our intercourse during the later months. I was occasionally bothered by shortness of breath during intercourse, but that was more of a nuisance than anything else."

• "As I am fortunate to have a happy marriage and had three healthy pregnancies, sex during

these periods was as enjoyable and natural as ever. It is a fact that the last two months stimulated our imagination to get around the little somebody between us; the conventional positions provoked lots of kicking from the baby, and the female-dominant position gave rise to muscle spasms—however, I took pleasure in satisfying my husband without penetration during that short time."

• "Once my belly got too large (which really didn't happen until the seventh month), I turned to the side and my husband entered from behind. This he found less stimulating, although I did not."

The big belly and greater fatigue of the last months of pregnancy do not have to be insurmountable. These obstacles can show the way to imaginative new discoveries which are often most satisfying. Experimentation in pregnancy can lead not only to new positions, but also to new pleasuring and caressing that enhance the joy and closeness of a couple.

• "The last months of pregnancy forced us to try new positions in sex, which was good— creatures of habit that we are after six years. We openly discussed what was best for each."

• "Although we were reassured that it was okay to have sex right up to the last, I think from past experience we have both been slightly brainwashed as to the dangers of infection. When I was diagnosed as being 75 percent effaced, and who knew when dilation might begin, we

stopped. Or rather he stopped, as I for some reason became more interested in experimenting with different nonvaginal methods. After several frustrating attempts, we found a mutual masturbation technique that accomplished something of what we were after. I think this was an important discovery, as by a necessity it has opened our horizons, so to speak, for further sexual communication. I think that if sex is mutually satisfying but more or less the same every time, the relationship could become more commonplace than need be. In this, our third pregnancy, we finally discovered that there are alternatives—when all returns to normal, I think my husband and I will be in much closer communication than before."

• "Logistically it is difficult for us to have sex as often as we'd like . . . an increased amount of affection, just being touched or kissed, was often what I really wanted—at times much more than making love."

• "My desire for stimulating sexual activity was nonexistent but my need for vocal endearments and 'caring' little hugs and kisses increased."

Both men and women frequently seem to differentiate between making love and "just" being touched or kissed. Both of these two women are surprised at their desire for affection in general at a time when they are not interested in coitus. Surely the term "making love" can include all expressions of affection from caressing, touching, and kissing to intercourse, oral sex, and manual stimulation.

These shifts in the kind of affection that one or both partners desire can place a new stress on the relationship. Communication and mutual caring can be extremely important to help the couple work out their priorities.

- "Some of our favorite positions were no longer comfortable for me. However, our priorities were firmly set in being together; and a less appealing position did not seem a problem or lessen our pleasure. My 'roundness' was often cause for a good laugh as we tried to maneuver our 'family' into a comfortable arrangement. This was a minor inconvenience. Our emphasis was on the much-wanted baby. I used to stand in front of our bedroom door mirror at some point each day or evening—my husband's study is also in the bedroom—and we would both enjoy my changing shape. Sometimes we would dance and he would good-humoredly suck his belly in to make room for mine. We used to laugh and say one concave needs the other convex. Yes, I think you could say our pregnancy was sexual—it was also very tender-making and very provider-affirming."

- "The period of abstinence, which I remember as being longer than my wife remembers, posed no problem for me. There were too many new excitements, too many other loving things to do together, like feeling and watching the little kicks, like admiring the magnificent abdominal roundness, like glorying in the incredible softness of maternal skin and flesh, the shining of maternal eyes and maternal smile."

• "Our solution to not having intercourse was to become physically close without necessarily having sex. We concentrated on lying together or snuggling as we called it, massaging each other. We found that this approach made us very relaxed and much closer than we had been for a very long time, even before we conceived. We felt open and warm and loving to each other. It also allowed us to get in touch with our unborn child together and very involved in the approaching birth."

Not all problems of lovemaking in pregnancy are as obviously physical as those associated with the awkwardness of a large belly and the fatigue of the body. Even couples who feel that their sexual relationships remained wonderful up to the last moments of the pregnancy admit to some difficulties. These are thoughtfully expressed by several women:

• "Physically I was at the maximum of discomfort, and mentally there was so much concentration on myself and my baby that anything and anybody at that point was an intrusion. My husband's attitude at this time can best be described as sympathetic to the cause."

• "Sex really seemed relatively unimportant. I felt most of my energies going into the baby—mentally and physically—and getting our home ready. I seemed to have a real homing instinct. This did not present any conflict between me and my husband. My body feels somehow introverted or preoccupied and doesn't always respond, causing occasional friction between my

husband and myself. As I felt this was psychological and presumably terminal with the birth
of the baby, I did not seek medical advice."

This same feeling of inwardness and self-
absorption is given a different interpretation by a
woman whose husband did not want to have sexual relations with her after her body was visibly
pregnant:

• **"Perhaps a kind of self-involved sensuality—sexuality was my way of avoiding
frustration in the last trimester. We stopped a
bit earlier in our second pregnancy than we had
in our first, at the beginning of the seventh
month, perhaps because I was expecting it and
did not prod."**

In addition to the withdrawal and the concern
with the most important project—making a
baby—making love could be affected by feelings
about the changes in the woman's body—not just
the physical awkwardness, but the actual meaning
of her big belly, swollen breasts, and changed
chemistry.

Our cultural attitudes and personal self image
often affect our reactions. It is easy to understand
one woman who said, "How can anything so big be
sexy?" Others have remarked:

• **"My husband found me physically less desirable, and purely objectively, I think that is natural. We both found intimacy and excitement
through oral sex—but abstinence from intercourse for a long time eventually was very hard
on both of us, physically and emotionally."**

- "My main fear before pregnancy was an aesthetic one. I have lived with a terror that obesity is just around the corner and that J., who is thin and handsome, would abandon me if I ever let myself go. . . . I have to admit that, to me, many pregnant women look like cows. It's not nice to say, but I have never subscribed to the theory that during pregnancy a woman becomes her most beautiful—although people do tend to tell you that a lot."

- "Around the middle of the eighth month, I began to feel particularly ungainly and unattractive, although he kept protesting that it wasn't so. The frequency of our relations declined—when we did have sex, I enjoyed it thoroughly."

- "Because I knew my body brought M. no visual pleasure, I often arranged to be under the covers when he came to bed."

It is difficult to say whether the woman's feelings about her body elicited the husband's negative response or whether it was his attitude and preconceived notion of feminine beauty that made her feel unlovely.

- "Later on, as sexy as I felt, it started to get harder for me to reach orgasm. I think it's because my mind was working overtime, and I knew my husband was repelled by my body (the stretch marks, and the big belly) even if he did make love to me. Because he thought I was an ugly body to be in, I felt ugly and angry at the baby for making me ugly."

92

- "At the end, I felt my body to be repulsive. My husband claimed he did not find me so, but he was definitely not turned on. Around the sixth month we went from having sex every other night to once or twice a week. This did nothing to help my unkind thoughts about myself or my increased desire. However, the one or two encounters a week were usually good experiences, and they kept us feeling warm and close about each other."

One husband said:

- "I do not subscribe to the old saw that women are more beautiful when they are pregnant; by and large, I think the opposite is true. However, the particular woman of whom I write has remained exceptionally beautiful throughout her pregnancy, and I have no complaints."

Obviously, this man saw more in his wife than just a big belly. What would normally have been a turn-off became meaningful and therefore a pleasure.

Another man was more ambivalent:

- "For some reason I became progressively more turned off as her pregnancy continued. There is no division by trimester, just a gradual development. It might be that K. was fifty pounds over her ideal weight, but that is certainly not the whole story. I think my biggest problem was her deviation from the commercially acceptable image of womanhood, readily

available to anyone in today's press. Swollen bellies, swollen ankles, awkward carriage just don't measure up. Fantasies of women with stretch marks from pregnancy, loose vaginal muscles from childbirth, and sagging breasts from nursing didn't help matters. My sexual conditioning—and this is to a large extent everyone's sexual conditioning—just didn't allow for the realities of childbirth. It's strange that I always love the look of pregnant women, the proud carriage—proud, not awkward, when it's some other woman—the shining eyes, etc. With K., I couldn't see these things. I sometimes enjoyed seeing her sitting at home with my baby in her belly, but this was a family feeling, and maybe one of masculine pride in his brood; not a sexual feeling."

The wife of another man remarks:

• "My husband had an increased interest toward other women, with nice shapes, and less desire to have sex with me. I had no desire for sex during the last half of pregnancy."

The concept of beauty is a cultural variable. The voluptuous Venus of Willendorf portrayed the essence of beauty in 30,000 B.C. The graceful Venus de Milo was the ideal of womanhood in ancient Greece. Today, our female model seems to fluctuate between the unisex image and the soft peasant look.

Some couples, fortunately, are able to transcend the cultural stereotypes of what is "sexy" or attractive. They find beauty in the fullness of the pregnant figure and come together in the joy of their bodies and the delight of experiencing all the changes involved in growing a child.

- "During the late months, I was happily surprised that I did feel sexual; I did appeal to my husband; and our experiences were mutually satisfying. I became much more aggressive during this period because I felt extremely secure in our relationship. My husband's desire decreased considerably during this period. With the chemical change in my body, he detected a change in scent. We worked on this together by discussing things and realizing that it was a temporary situation. This way we alleviated mistaken assumptions and (most) hurt feelings."

- "When I was first pregnant, I worried that my husband would not like my body and that it would not feel good to him as I grew larger. The reverse happened. Every night he would study me and as the baby began to move we would watch the "show" for as much as half an hour every night. My belly was another part of me that he loved and my early fears were in vain. I adored my large belly and delighted in sharing the fetal movement with women at work who were curious. For the first time in my life, I had no feeling of awkwardness or dissatisfaction with my body. In fact, this seems to be one of the main things about pregnancy for me—that my feelings about my body underwent a tremendous positive change."

• "The fact that I never felt as though my husband considered me unattractive physically when I was pregnant influenced my entire attitude and pleasure in sex. He made me feel that I was still desirable to him."

In our culture it is difficult to connect the image of mother with the idea of sexual desire and sexual activity. It is hard for us to conceive that our own parents made love, even though we are the visible proof that they did. One father quoted above made the definite distinction between his "family feeling" and his "sexual feeling." The idea of the Madonna and the Immaculate Conception is our cultural heritage, leaving us with the feeling that when a woman is involved in childbearing she should not be associated with sexuality. The ideal of a "pure" madonna is related to incest taboos; if this is "mother"—my mother—even the thought of sexual relations with her is forbidden.

• "My husband found himself unable to approach me at around six months to term. He claimed he felt differently toward me as I was now a 'mother.' We made love very infrequently. I was not upset as I found it cumbersome, and I can go for long periods abstaining with no apparent distress. I felt somewhat upset by his decrease in physical attention but felt understanding and not really rejected."

• "I found it difficult to have my body function both as a sexpot and as a mother."
"Sometimes I felt I was not so desirable sexually because I was almost a mother—

fantasies about sexuality and motherhood not being compatible—but my husband has felt increased desire for me—finds me beautiful and is excited about what's going on in my body."

The husband's feelings are seldom given much attention in pregnancy. Too often it is taken to be the woman's unique experience. The fact is, however, that men are going through as many emotional—if not physical—changes as their wives. They too are becoming parents. A man must come to grips with the new family and social roles of being a parent. He must take on a new financial burden and live with a woman who is being transformed before his very eyes. He may enjoy the freedom of making love without contraceptives, but he may be appalled at the idea of his wife having a baby inside her uterus. A woman can feel the changes taking place within her own body. A man can only guess at what it must be like. He, too, may wish he could be so miraculously creative. He may feel himself identifying with the feminine, nurturant, maternal qualities he sees in his wife, but these qualities may feel alien to his increasing responsibilities as a man.

The husband may wish that his wife's body would stay as it was. Her new superfeminine body, her heavier scent, her extra lubrication, and her increased engorgement may be frightening, almost overwhelming. He may feel as though there is no more room for him inside his wife, or as though she is so engorged and lubricated that there is too much room. Either of these feelings can make a man lose his erection during lovemaking. Her fertile womanliness may make him feel temporarily pressured and inadequate.

Even if he is very excited about the pregnancy and likes the changes in his wife's body, a man may not want his well established patterns of lovemaking to be modified. Often, it is easier for him to find a non-pregnant woman to turn to rather than have to deal with making love to his pregnant wife. He may want to run away from the wife and baby and leave them to take care of themselves. Even if he does not literally leave, he may withdraw emotionally, perhaps feeling "kicked out" by the fetus.

If a man is brave enough to stay in touch with his wife during pregnancy, he may discover that he does not like the alternative methods of lovemaking suggested by books like this one. The American ideal of the male in the mid 1970s may include sexual sophistication and experimentation, but in fact, new forms of sexual behavior are not easy for anybody, man or woman. A lot depends on cultural attitudes and what was learned in childhood and adolescence. Mutual masturbation may feel regressive and unclean, like something that only kids should be doing, something that was okay as a teenager, but inappropriate to a married man about to become a father. A man (or a woman) may feel embarrassed about relaxing and enjoying sensual pleasure for its own sake. A husband may feel guilty about receiving sexual gratification when his wife does not want any for herself. Or a man may feel suddenly inadequate if his wife has rapid orgasms and he does not.

More gymnastic postures may be embarrassing to a man or may feel appropriate only with other women, certainly not with a mother-to-be, or a wife. And a man may have a deep-seated fear that if he tries these exotic postures, he may fail at them. Perhaps he has a fantasy that his penis is not big enough or that his erection is not firm enough to satisfy a woman in any but the tried-and-true position. Or he may feel that his body is not handsome enough for a woman to want to caress or look at during lovemaking. He may need as much gentle reassurance about not looking like Burt Reynolds as she does for not looking like Miss America.

Again and again it is the couple who can talk even about these frightening and personal feelings that make it through pregnancy with a stronger, deeper, and more trusting relationship. Men and women who pretend that nothing is going on miss the opportunity to grow closer together and learn new levels of relating and new depths of personal feelings.

Conflicts, fears, and tensions are difficult to avoid. They recur and persist even in wanted pregnancies and in warm, wonderful relationships. Some of them can be attributed to cultural attitudes, carry-overs from old wives' tales, upbringing, and attitudes inherited from our parents. For example, many couples are afraid they will infect the passage when they make love. Even some doctors prescribe abstinence in the final months and give this as their reason. Yet all the studies show that this fear is unfounded; sexual intercourse does not introduce an infection to the baby that is safely protected by an unbroken bag of fluid on the other side of a closed cervix. Healthy couples are no more likely to have problems with infections in pregnancy than at other times.

Similarly, medical science has assured us that the fetus is safe within the mother's body, that it is well protected in the uterus, enveloped in its sac, surrounded by water which acts as an excellent shock absorber. There is the bony pelvis to guard the body, the spine, the back, and the abdominal muscles and fat and layers of skin all to help. Most couples who go to childbirth education classes learn all this; many, many women are given the same assurance by their doctors. And yet the fears persist. Will sexual intercourse harm the baby? This anxiety is so close to universal that it is probably far deeper than just a rational concern.

• **"My husband really believed that he could harm the baby, and sometimes he expressed the fear that the baby could see him come inside me. We abstained for one month prior to delivery because of this."**

• **"I did worry somewhat that we would crush the baby. I had wondered if too heavy a bounce would hurt the baby—but I have basic faith in nature, so that was a passing thought."**

• **"In the back of our minds we felt that we might hurt the baby if we were too active during intercourse, so we sort of took it easy and changed positions."**

• **"I must honestly say that I did have somewhat of a guilty feeling and fear of something happening to my unborn child because of my sexual feelings. I was not able to fully enjoy sexual relations with my husband. He, however, was not aware of my fears (I didn't tell him) and was quite happy and satisfied with our relationship."**

Some husbands are more concerned than their wives:

101

- "I was afraid to damage the fetus late in pregnancy. No one really told us what the actual chances of such damage were, and unexpected fears have a way of taking larger proportions than they deserve. These fears, rational or irrational, seemed to affect feelings about sex and the relationship with my partner."

- "The last time we had sex before our son's birth was five days before—by then (the very last weeks) my husband was very gentle, saying he didn't want to hurt the baby."

- "In the third trimester, my husband became resistant to having intercourse for fear of hurting the baby. This was especially the case when the doctor told me the baby was in the head-down position. However, since we had developed an enjoyable pattern of alternatives and since my clitoris has always been more stimulating than my vagina, no problems developed. I felt it was my feminist obligation, however, to tell him time and time again that intercourse was not harmful to the baby's head."

- "One hang-up for me was the proximity of K.'s genitals to the fetus. It's almost as if you wake the baby. Someone should tell people that the fetus is safely and securely separated from the genitals and totally disinterested in what is going on out there."

This father had been told that he could not hurt the baby, and yet he stayed worried, perhaps because babies often **do** react to lovemaking.

Babies characteristically respond to sound waves, to the movements of their mother. (Some babies seem to "go to sleep" when the mother is up and about and very active, and to "wake up" and move and kick and "go for a walk" the moment she sits down and relaxes, or tries to sleep, or takes a nice, relaxing bath.)

• **"The baby seemed to object or approve of its father's most definite presence by kicking, squirming, or causing an enormous Braxton-Hicks contraction afterwards. We both thought that was funny."**

Some couples are disconcerted by all the activity inside of the uterus. When the baby kicks and squirms during or after lovemaking, they become aware of its presence and begin to worry that their behavior may be inappropriate.

• **"Sometimes baby would kick a lot, and I'd feel there was someone present who really shouldn't be there—and it was a bit disturbing."**

While the baby's movements may be a reaction to what is going on around it, by its getting jolted and rocked as the mother participates in sexual activity, the baby is not causing the uterine contractions. The uterus itself is responding to the mother's orgasm, as it does even in the nonpregnant state. These contractions of the uterus will not hurt the baby, nor will they normally cause the mother to go into premature labor.

• **"I had an orgasm during my sixth month which caused my belly to contract. I was scared**

I was hurting the baby or doing something wrong. I told my doctor and he assured me that these uterine contractions would not hurt the baby or bring on labor before I was ready."

These long-lasting uterine spasms after an orgasm are considered quite normal during pregnancy.

- "Sometimes after orgasm I had an almost painful uterine contraction—which went away almost immediately—so I would think I was bringing on labor—but so far, it hasn't worked, which is too bad because I'm two days past my due date and am anxious to have my baby."

- "After my orgasm, the uterus seemed to go through incredible contortions of readjustment or something—I was unable to move for a full five minutes each time."

The resolution period of the sexual arousal cycle takes much longer during pregnancy than at other times. The uterus may stay hard for several minutes, particularly late in the pregnancy of a woman who has been pregnant before. One woman noted this phenomenon for the first time and remarked that it "somehow escaped me in previous pregnancies." It may in fact not have occurred in previous pregnancies, as the slow resolution is related to the amount of engorgement in the genitals and seems to become more pronounced as each subsequent pregnancy progresses.

The normal increase in the blood flow to the genital area which is typical of sexual arousal as well as pregnancy causes feelings of fullness and swelling. While it can be frustrating and uncomfortable in its advanced stages, it also accounts for heightened sensitivity and more frequent orgasms in some women:

- "The final three months I have experienced a heightening of sexual enjoyment. Whereas before we could rate sexual experiences on perhaps a 1 (routine) to 5 (very passionate) scale of intensity (depending on mood beforehand, degree of fatigue, etc., I would say that after the sixth month our sexual relations have maintained a higher plateau of intensity, regardless of mood or fatigue. Almost every time I experience multiple (two or three) orgasms, which is not unusual but not the norm for me, either. This is another reason, I'm certain, why we decided not to give up sex during the ninth month—whatever feels good can't be bad.

"As for orgasms, I've had no fear of their hurting the fetus. I figure they're basically contractions and, if anything, they strengthen the muscles and are beneficial rather than detrimental. If in the ninth month they encourage the baby to come sooner, then they don't make any difference one way or another. I think people who say orgasms aren't good would also say that masturbation causes insanity, hairy palms, and pimples."

Medical opinion is still mixed as to whether or not an orgasm can sometimes initiate premature labor. Since it does cause the uterus to contract, a woman with a particularly sensitive uterus or a history of trouble carrying a baby to full term might be asked to try to avoid having an orgasm. But it is apparent from our study and others that most women who enjoy both intercourse and orgasm to the very end of their pregnancy do so without complications.

The engorgement of the genitals that often heightens pleasure during intercourse may also cause discomfort and an increased discharge from the vagina which can affect sexual relations adversely.

• **"My husband stopped having oral-genital sex because he didn't like the discharge."**

• **"My vagina seems so swollen that it almost feels as if my body is trying to 'push out' my husband's penis; it's like there is no room for him in there anymore."**

• **"My genitals seemed enlarged most of the time. I never heard anything about this, but I just assume that others experience it, too, and that it is normal."**

The sexual response cycle of a woman who is not pregnant follows the general pattern of gradually increasing lubrication and engorgement during the arousal phase, culminating in orgasm, followed by gradual dispersal of the extra blood in the genital area and cessation of the extra lubrication during the resolution phase. If the couple has been given no restrictions on intercourse late in pregnancy, they will find that the genitals remain engorged with an increased blood supply even after orgasm. Some women find themselves compulsively seeking orgasmic release but never achieving the condi-

106

tion for which they hope, no matter how many orgasms they experience. Other women stop trying to have orgasms because they report a decreased intensity and satisfaction in the experience during the last two or three months of pregnancy. This, added to the difficulties associated with feeling unlovely or unloved and the purely physical problem of being clumsy, can make it very difficult for a woman to relax enough to reach orgasm. Additionally, as labor and delivery approach, some women experience acute anxiety about the birth itself and about whether or not they will be adequate mothers. They know their life is out of control and they are afraid. This fear of loss of control can become a generalized tension that affects sexual responsiveness. Orgasm may be experienced by a woman as an "opening up" and as a "letting go." She may be afraid to do either.

When a woman wants to be orgasmic but finds that she is having trouble reaching orgasm, she can become even more tense and anxious, thus making it even more difficult for her to enjoy sensuality, to participate in lovemaking, and to have an orgasm. The strong-willed desire for an orgasm may itself inhibit the chances of achieving one. During pregnancy as at other times, lovemaking is in danger of being ruined by being made too goal-oriented. When a man and woman come together to take pleasure from each other's bodies, to caress their beloved and to receive sensual pleasure, they will be making love, whether or not either achieves orgasm. However, it may be reassuring for a woman to know that the rate of orgasms often declines during the last trimester of pregnancy. Wagner and Solberg report that before conception, half of the women they studied reported achieving

107

orgasm at least 76 percent of the time. In the ninth month of pregnancy, only 23 percent of their women achieved orgasm that often; 57 percent achieved orgasm 24 percent or less of the time. In other words, the majority of women they studied said that they only had orgasms one out of every four times they had coitus in the last trimester even though the majority had achieved orgasms three out of four times they had coitus before pregnancy. [12]

Most of the factors that are inhibiting orgasms in pregnant women will disappear when the pregnancy is over. However, the relationship between the man and woman and the fact of parenthood do not go away. The postpartum period contains no magic; it brings problems of its own. Any time a woman is worried about orgasms, like any time a man is worried about achieving erections, the best treatment is to create a relaxed, non-demanding environment in which she (he) feels truly loved and cared for.

It will be difficult but important for couples to work out their relationships fairly, acknowledging very real fears, not overreacting to old wives' tales, understanding each other's anxieties, being able to openly discuss problems and work out solutions which will help their love and their intimate relationship.

● **"I think that most couples would like to and even try having sex until the end except for all those old wives' tales and passed down fears of older generations. My mother made me promise not to take a bath or swim while I was pregnant, probably because it was unheard of in her**

108

day. I guess some things will never change, no matter even if they are medically proven."

• "At our six-weeks-before-birth-day mark, I felt some apprehension as I could feel the baby's head lowering somewhat. My doctor said that abstention during the last month is quite common, but that it's not harmful to continue right to the end of pregnancy, as long as the husband's penetration was shallow. That sounded a bit tricky to me as my husband is very well endowed. But also I've found very little sex drive in me at this point and my husband seems to adjust to this brilliantly, just as he did in our last pregnancy. If this poses any problem for him, he's doing a remarkable job of not showing it."

• "Besides needing my own sexual fulfillment, I think I must have harked back subconsciously at first to some friends who had a baby several years ago. The woman apparently experienced a decrease in sexual desire and her partner, during her pregnancy, had an affair with another woman. I always thought this was dreadful, that during this remarkable time a couple should turn their backs on each other. (They've since divorced.) I decided consciously beforehand that if I experienced a decrease in sexual desire I was going to work through it somehow and not give in to it. Even though I'd read that many women feel sexier than ever during pregnancy, I never thought it would happen to me because I thought I'd be miserable with a big fat belly. As it turned out, I really got into the whole experience much more than I thought I would, and I have definitely felt physically more stimulated more often during these last months."

Many doctors will not put any restrictions whatsoever on sexual activities during pregnancy unless there are medical reasons, in which case they will specify whether either intercourse or orgasm has to be restricted. It is advisable to discuss sexual activities during pregnancy with the doctor, if only to be reassured.

While concerns of the pregnant couple are understandable, they are often unrelated to actual factors of health or safety. Sometimes they even become irrational:

• "I'm nervous every time I make love to my wife because I keep thinking maybe the baby can bite me."

• "I found that my sexual desires heightened after my fourth month of pregnancy and continued until the end of my eighth month. My orgasms were stronger and lasted longer than usual. I experienced guilt feelings for the sexual act because I felt that any abnormal sexual behavior to surface later on in my baby's life would be directly attributable to my increased feelings at this time.

"I would attribute the diminution in sex drive only partly to the physical discomfort and more to the psychological stress. I think it was due to several ill-defined factors such as being sick and tired of walking around in maternity clothes which I began, by then, to view as a kind of uniform; being disgruntled with the fact of

110

having great difficulty in performing as simple a task as cutting my toenails; having to resort to ingenuity for getting out of bed in the morning; and feeling—as irrational as that seemed even at the time—that I was doomed to remain in that state forever. All of which were complemented by my anticipation of the arrival of my hopefully healthy child. There constantly lurked in my mind the fear that my child would be born less than completely healthy."

Some couples complain that advice from doctors has been scanty and arbitrary. Because sexual behavior is a sensitive topic, some doctors will not introduce the subject unless the woman asks for specific advice. A number of doctors still routinely tell their patients to abstain from intercourse in the last six weeks or last month without saying why. Frequently the woman and her partner are too shy to question such a dictum, though others follow their own feelings and instincts. It may be advisable to consult your doctor in any case. A couple who ignores the prohibition may be taking an unnecessary risk while those who follow it without understanding why may be putting unnecessary strain on their marital relationship.

• "I ignored the doctor and enjoyed having both my husband and my baby inside of me at the same time."

• "Sex was never mentioned by our doctor—I didn't mention it because I was afraid he would tell us to abstain. Therefore after each visit to the doctor the 'no news is good news' policy was our guideline. It would have been helpful if the

111

doctor had said something; my husband and I would have felt less that each time we were together was perhaps 'The Last Hurrah.' "

- "The fact that I'm pregnant hasn't really changed the way we make love or feel about sex. Once over the 'delicate condition' fallacy, thanks to long talks and my exercise classes, we realized I could reach to the second kitchen shelf as well as make love without walking on eggshells. I've suffered no physical discomfort during intercourse, and we can still enjoy the positions we always enjoyed. My husband had mentioned once that when the baby is bigger and perhaps less padded, we might hurt it during intercourse. I told him I thought the bigger it is, the stronger it is, too, and I really didn't think it should be a worry. He never mentioned it again and seems to have put it out of his mind."

Not all couples experience pregnancy as an obstacle to their sexual expression:

- "I always thought that one experienced sex in spite of being pregnant, never in terms of pregnancy as being a sexual experience. As I said, I just don't think that we're very aware of the fetus when we're making love. But if you look at the experience as a whole, after nine months I guess I'd have to agree that pregnancy might really be the ultimate sexual experience. I've really liked being pregnant a lot more than I thought I would. Right now, though, all I can think of is having that baby. The Lamaze classes have really taught me a lot about my

112

body and taken away the fear of childbirth, since most of the fear on my part was based on ignorance of what was happening to me and what was going to happen once I got to the hospital. Now I'm really looking forward to the birth and all the physical aspects of it, and I don't think that would have happened without the classes. The classes also contributed to our relaxed attitude towards sex in the last month."

It is difficult to summarize the joys, anxieties, difficulties, and solutions experienced by men and women in the last three months of pregnancy because they are often so contradictory and based on highly individual responses to a more general phenomena. The following account gives a balanced view of many of the common experiences:

• "My husband and I enjoyed sex throughout my pregnancy, although I think we were both very much aware of my being pregnant, and at times this seemed to somewhat lessen the 'concentration' of making love. By this I mean that sex was now a bit different—my body was 'different' in that it was carrying on a totally new function. As I became closer to the delivery date—actually the last few months and also especially during the first few months of the postpartum—I found it difficult to have my body function both as a sex partner and as a mother. I was extremely interested in childbearing and in the entire birth process; I read extensively on the subject, and the more I read, the more it seemed as though my body was really performing a function so completely marvelous that nothing else relating to my body

113

mattered—including sex. Everything was for the baby. At times I just found it difficult psychologically to have sex and carry a child at the same time.

"On the other hand, there were times—even in the last few months before delivery—when I felt a great affection for my husband, almost to the extent where I felt the baby was an 'intruder' on these last few weeks of only my husband and myself making up our 'family.' Looking back, I guess I had these feelings of ambivalence and mood swings throughout my pregnancy, and I never could figure out just why I would switch so quickly from one end of the spectrum to the other.

"However, I think any psychological effect was lesser than the physical one—when we did have intercourse, it was good and I never experienced any physical discomfort at all. I never had any fears that the child would abort because of intercourse, but I did worry somewhat that we would 'crush' the baby. But as my stomach expanded, we tried new positions, and I didn't worry about it anymore."

No one person can speak for all, yet this woman clearly reflects the frequently expressed sense that even when pregnancy is a happy, joyous experience, worries and conflicts occur. The transformations of the last months are simply too profound to ignore. A willingness to understand what is going on, to experiment with new ways of expressing mutual love, and to discuss problems and feelings with their partners seem to be even more helpful for young couples during pregnancy than at other time in their marriage.

Labor and Delivery

Many people may find it strange to think of labor and delivery as having anything to do with making love. However, the process of giving birth is inextricably bound to acts of love not only because the infant was conceived during an act of sexual union, but also because the mother's and father's ongoing care is a fundamental expression of love. Birth is a moment in time poised between the sexual love of mother and father and the nurturant love of parents for child.

Childbirth is more than the act of receiving a new person into the family. It is a challenging and stressful process. The woman's body goes through extraordinary changes that involve her in experiences she has never had at any other time. She may wonder whether or not she can do it. She must be taken care of by the people around her. Increasingly in our society she turns to her husband for support through the crisis, for he is as involved in the creation and care of the child as she. Even more, he may have been her closest confidant during the pregnancy. He is the one who has shared her most intimate moments of fear, wonder, and joy. He has lived with her changing body and helped her get ready for the new child. When things are going well, she may feel that she is doing it all for him; when they are going badly, she may blame

115

him for getting her into this. In either case, he is the object of her strong feelings. He cannot escape the knowledge of his role as lover, husband, and father-to-be.

When a man chooses to stay by his wife through labor and birth, and when she asks him to be with her, the couple is expressing its faith in their love. Labor is always physically and emotionally stressful, even when it is a fast and "easy" birth. There are many loving things a husband can do to make it easier for his wife. He can chat with her to help pass the time, check out her muscles to keep her relaxed, lead her in her breathing to ease the way through contractions, keep her attention focused when the sensations of the baby passing through the birth canal become greater than she could have believed. He can offer her ice chips, call the nurse, massage her back, help her stay comfortable through an internal examination, praise her, encourage her, correct her performance—in short, he can take care of her. Surely all these things are acts of love.

Sometimes a man does not feel comfortable in the role of caretaker and a woman resents having to be taken care of. They may not like the roles they are forced to take at this time. But these roles are part of our biological heritage. A woman in childbirth is vulnerable and cannot defend herself; her mate becomes her protector. The couples who

I. The position of the organs inside a woman's pelvis. In the unaroused state, the vagina is a **potential** rather than an actual space.

116

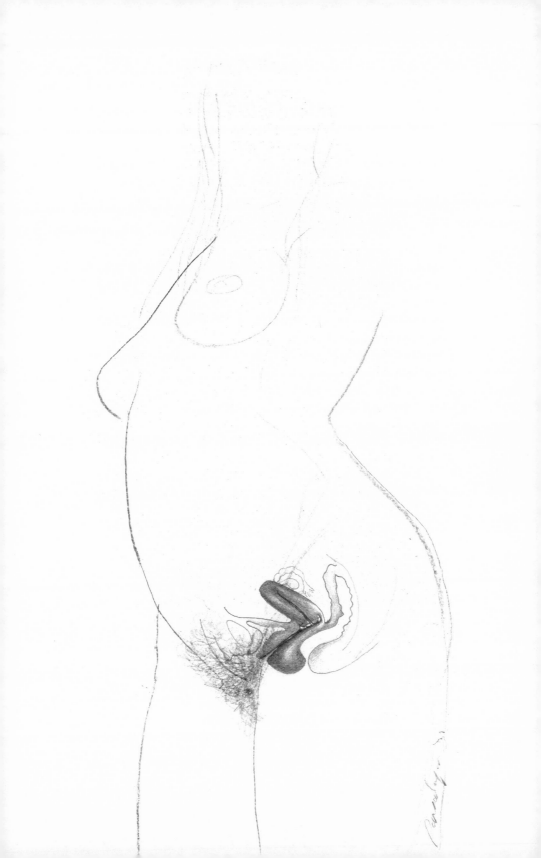

realize this and who accept the changes can come through the experience with deepened trust of each other and of themselves.

Women who have had to work hard to expel their baby may have trouble imagining that birth could ever be a sensual experience, akin to lovemaking. A large baby moving inch by inch down a small vagina causes so much pressure that the sensation is unrelated to stimulation of the same areas under other circumstances. And yet, physiologically, there are parallels between giving birth and making love. The same hormones, organs and responses are involved in both: the area becomes engorged with blood; the vagina lubricates and opens; and the genitals go through rhythmic spasm (three to twelve throbs in the case of orgasm; hours of regular and progressively stronger contractions in the case of birth). Stimulation of breasts and other erogenous zones releases oxytocin and makes both experiences progress more rapidly.

In an article called "Interrelationships between Sexual Responsiveness, Birth, and Breast Feeding," Niles Newton analyzes the comparison between undisturbed, undrugged childbirth and sexual excitement.[13] She remarks on eleven specific characteristics:

1. Changes in breathing;
2. A tendency to make vocal noises;

II. During sexual arousal, the vagina becomes an **actual** space. Enlarged and lubricated, the vagina can comfortably receive a penis.

118

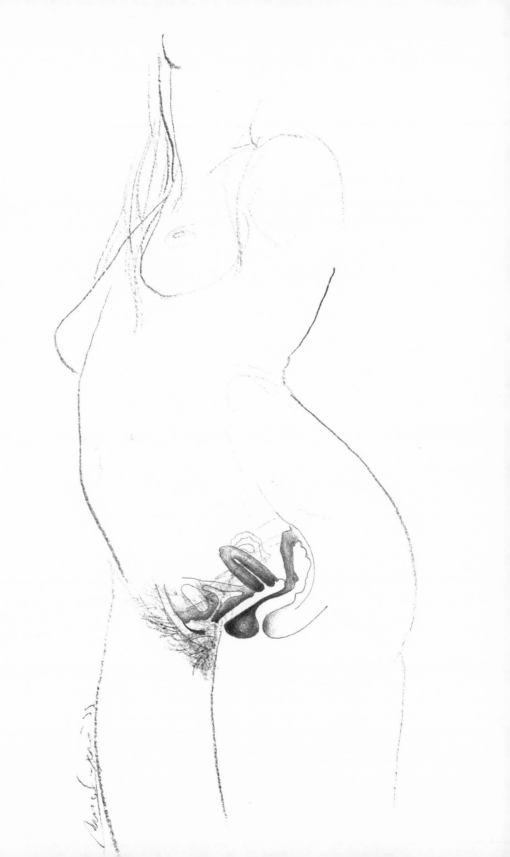

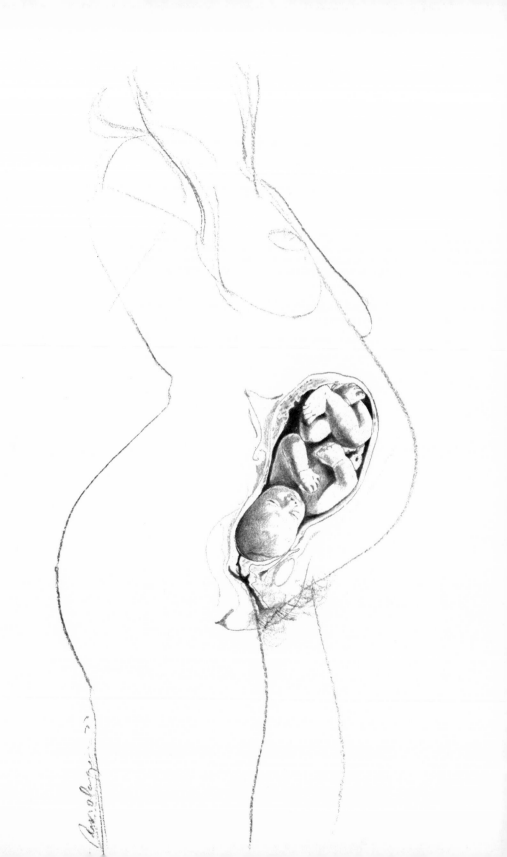

3. Facial expressions reminiscent of an athlete under great strain;
4. Rhythmic contractions of the upper segment of the uterus;
5. Loosening of the mucus plug from the os of the cervix;
6. Periodic abdominal muscle contractions;
7. Use of a position in which the woman is on her back with her legs wide apart and bent;
8. A tendency to become uninhibited;
9. Unusual muscular strength;
10. A tendency to be unaware of the world and a sudden return to alert awareness after climax or birth;
11. A feeling of joy and well being following the climax or birth.

These objective, observable phenomena are reinforced by the subjective experiences of many women who have given birth while undisturbed and undrugged. Masters and Johnson learned that some women who have had babies (and none who had not) describe the sensation of imminent or-

III. During pregnancy, the vagina still goes through stages of enlargement with sexual arousal. When the cervix remains intact, the baby is well separated from the vagina. In preparation for delivery, the cervix effaces and dilates and the vagina enlarges enough to accommodate the passage of the baby through the birth canal. The vagina returns to being a potential space soon after delivery. It will enlarge again during sexual arousal.

gasm as "a feeling of receptive opening."[14] Twelve women in their study who had given birth without anesthesia or analgesia "reported that the second stage of labor felt like the sensations just before orgasm, but greatly exaggerated."

Both sex and childbirth are experienced as life's greatest pleasures by some women and as its greatest burden by others.

• **"I enjoyed the sensations involved with being pregnant and dreamed about giving birth, which was the sexual experience of my life. (It wasn't so much this time, because of the nature of my labor, but it was with my first baby.)"**

This was written by a woman who experienced heightened desire all through pregnancy. Her problem was trying to get her husband to stay interested in having sex.

Another woman tells a very different story:

• **"I found during the third trimester of pregnancy I preferred to sleep by myself. The only time I wanted my husband to touch me was when I wanted to have sex. The same day I was admitted to the hospital to have my baby, my sexual desire became stronger than it had been in my life. Then the sexual desire went away when I saw the blood from my mucus plug."**

It is probably that this woman inhibited her sexual feelings because she felt them to be inappropriate during labor.

Some women express an awareness of a relationship between sexuality and giving birth even

122

when they do not experience birth itself as an arousing, sensual event.

- **"My last pregnancy was my third, therefore I was not nervous anymore. In my first two pregnancies I experienced a lot of bleeding, so we tried to restrain from sex a little. In my third pregnancy I did not have any bleeding, so we did not have to restrain. As my pregnancy went on our feelings were intensified; we both enjoyed orgasms each time. I think having sex until the end of my pregnancy led to a good delivery at the end."**

- **"If all women in labor could be treated like adults, with a little encouragement, they might not mind having babies or sex."**

Niles Newton believes that sexual intercourse, giving birth, and nursing are closely interrelated:

> In practical terms, this implies that what occurs on the delivery table is very pertinent to what will transpire later in the marital bed. . . . It is of biological and clinical significance that coitus, birth, and lactation appear to have a common neurohormonal base and share the tendency to be inhibited by environmental disturbance. All three appear, under some circumstances, to trigger caretaking behavior, which is an essential part of mammalian reproduction. . . .[15]

As discussed in the last chapter, most couples experience a decreased interest in sexual intercourse in the last weeks of pregnancy. However, when some couples say that they made love right up to the end, they mean it quite literally:

- **"The only time I was told to abstain was at the rupture of membranes. I had sex until then."**

The idea of sexual behavior this late in pregnancy is controversial. Some doctors are concerned that through the man's orgasm and the hormone prostaglandin in his ejaculation, labor might be initiated prematurely, even though it has been shown that it would need far greater amounts of prostaglandin to cause the uterus to go into action than could be found in normal semen. At full term this obviously is not a problem, since the initiation of labor may be actively desired.

Lovemaking (perhaps excluding penetration of the vagina) during the early stages of labor can be a warm and reassuring way for a couple to spend their time. Stimulation of the breasts and other erogenous zones releases hormones that seem to speed up the pace of the labor. Massage of the external vagina or labia is prescribed by some doctors to help relax the skin and improve the elasticity of the area that must stretch as the baby passes through. Perhaps most importantly, the intimate interaction between husband and wife can give them a chance to work out anieties they have about each other and reaffirm their devotion to helping each other through the crisis.

The relationship between lovemaking and childbirth is hard to remember in the hospital environment and while the incredible process of labor is going on. Gentle effleurage (massage) of the lower abdomen and a good back rub are about all

124

the physical contact most couples care to engage in. But with the increased incidence of home birth and the evolution of family-centered maternity care, new attitudes are coming into play. Husbands and wives are realizing that their relationship does not cease as they enter the hospital and resume when they go out again. They are bringing all their intimate joys and possibly some of their petty angers to the hospital. Consequently, hospital staff members are beginning to learn more about the relationship between a man and a woman, lovemaking, and childbirth.

It is not unusual for women to resent the intrusion of their husbands on the essentially solitary experience of labor. As the force of the physical changes consume all a woman's energies, she may withdraw from the people around her. If she has had romantic notions about how she and her husband would stay in loving unison throughout the birth of their child, she may feel guilt at ignoring him:

• **"The first time I had thought I would go right through it gazing into his eyes, but when the baby started to descend, I just forgot he was there. All I cared about was getting that baby out. And then it came, and I just wanted to hold it. I had to remind myself that he was there and that I should share it with him. I felt kind of shocked when I realized how far from him, emotionally, I'd been. His being there just really didn't matter to me then. It took me months to admit that.**

"The second time, I told him to just enjoy it for himself, that I'd be busy with what I had to do. When the baby started to crown, he was

jumping up and down with excitement. I was furious. Here I was struggling hard while he was having a good time. We still chuckle about that one. When I think about it now it's unbelievable, how happy he was and what a beautiful baby we got. I worked hard, but then I was the one who got to hold the baby and put it to my breast. I wasn't jealous anymore."

Sheila Kitzinger, a well-known British author and childbirth educator, suggests that uterine inertia or malfunctioning of the uterus seems to occur more frequently among women who are characteristically "inhibited, embarrassed by the processes that were taking place in their bodies, ladylike in the extreme, and endured what they were undergoing stoically."[16] Women must be helped to relax and open up to give birth. She thinks the marital relationship is the best guide to whether or not this will happen. Some women need the security of the hospital to really feel trust and be able to relax. Others react with tension at the institution. For them the presence of their husbands can reduce anxiety that might otherwise keep their uterus from functioning as well as it could. The husband seems to help create a familiar psychological environment in the strange place and make it easier to relax.

For some women, the husband's presence makes it **more** difficult to relax. If she is afraid to open up because she is worried about what he will think of her if she really "lets go" or "opens up," she will have trouble relaxing. She might be better off without having him near.

Birth involves the sex organs, but it hardly

exposes a woman in a romantic light. She may be sweating profusely and contorting her face with exertion. Her labia and vagina are stretched to their limit, opening a passage large enough for the baby. This whole thing has been known to "turn off" a man. One wrote to Dear Abby that he was not able to make love to his wife after watching the birth of his child. It is easy to understand his reaction. Watching the extension of the vagina may be particularly distressing. He may have trouble believing that his wife's body will ever return to a form and size appropriate for the entry of his penis in lovemaking. He may think she will never again be like she was. But if he stops to think of the difference between her size before she has been sexually aroused and her size after they have enjoyed some love play, perhaps he will appreciate the wondrous nature of the vagina which can grow and shrink in a manner not unlike that of his own penis. If he can learn to appreciate the transformation of his wife's body, he can also help her accept what is happening. After all, she may be subject to the same fears that bother him:

- **"When the doctor was stitching me up, he remarked that he was "fixing me up" for my husband without any regard for the way I felt about my genitals. At that point all I could think of was 'Will I ever be the same again? Will it ever be the same again?' "**

Some wives would rather avoid the stress of birth. They cannot absent themselves, but they want to protect their husbands from this experience. One wrote:

127

Dear Abby:

I was glad to see that letter in your column from the husband who was completely "turned off" sex since watching the birth of his child. It just bears out what I've always maintained: when one's husband witnesses such an event, it's the end of the romance!

No one could ever persuade me to allow my husband in the delivery room. I agree with the letter; it's a sickening and revolting affair, but unfortunately that's the way all babies come into the world, so we just have to put up with it.

Just the same, I think it's ridiculous to try to make a "beautiful and fulfilling experience" out of something that is clearly ugly. I say, for goodness' sake, keep the husband **out** and away from the birth if you want to keep romance **in** your marriage.

I love my children, but I loathe the birth process.

MOTHER OF TWO

DEAR MOTHER: I've never regarded the birth process as "sickening and revolting," but ugliness—like beauty—lies in the eye of the beholder. So to each his own.[17]

A woman in hard labor does not have much in common with the cultural ideal represented by our modern fashion model. She is closer to the statues of the earth goddess, relics of prehistoric times. She is like the Hindu goddess Kali, the female creator/destroyer, or the Celtic Sheela-na-ga, or like the symbols of awesome female power from all over the world. She may be frighteningly different from her usual feminine appearance—not at all the girl he married. She may need to know, however, that she is still loved.

• "My labor had slowed down and almost stopped. Finally a new nurse came on duty. She got me on my feet and suggested I take a shower. After lying all night in that barren little room on that plain bed, it felt good to be standing naked with the water running over my body. Then suddenly the contractions started coming on in a whole new way. I was embarrassed because I was naked. R. was standing just outside the curtain and he asked if I was all right when he heard me change my breathing. I guess I didn't answer. Anyway, he opened the curtain. I was standing there, bent almost double, with a contraction just sweeping through my body. It didn't hurt, exactly, just kind of consumed me. And he said something like, 'My god, you look fantastic, like some kind of great earth goddess.' It really turned me around; I'd been feeling awkward and a little frightened, but suddenly it felt right, as though my bare body and dripping hair didn't matter, at least not in front of him. Then I had to go to the bathroom, urgently. I grabbed a towel and ran across the hall—of course it was the baby. My bowels had been empty for hours. She just came barreling on down. Apparently I went from six centimeters to full dilation just standing there in that shower. R. laughed when the nurse told me to get off the john and come to the labor bed to be

129

examined. Then everybody started running around in circles. They had to wake up the doctor and transfer me to the delivery room while I kept on blowing to hold the baby back. As soon as everything was in place I pushed. The head was hard, but then her little body just went 'schloooop!!' and there she was."

Cultural patterns are constantly changing. Many, many think that the birth of a child should be a shared experience, and even hospitals have shown efforts in the last few years to give couples the opportunity to be together during the birth of their child, and to welcome the father and provide comfort and dignity for both parents.

Dr. Philip Sumner of Manchester, Connecticut, is a pioneer for the concept of combining labor and delivery room. He offers in his hospital a colorful and homelike atmosphere in what he calls "The Lamaze Room," or ABC, alternative birth center. (Dr. Sumner says color has never been known to cause infection in childbirth.) He encourages the mother to labor in any way that is comfortable for her, sitting in a chair, in bed, lying on her side, kneeling, standing. Dr. Sumner says, "Childbirth should be like a wedding; just as personal and just as special." To make this possible, professionals must be able to adjust their technical expertise to the physical and also psychological changes inherent in working with a couple in a "Lamaze Room." They will have to show a great flexibility without losing their skill and personal sensitivity. When asked by a couple, whether he does not get bored helping so many people give birth, Dr. Sumner said, "It's like an actor who has to perform the same play night after night, but each time must be different because the participants are never the same."

At the same time, the couples must be willing to face their own fears about themselves and about their partners and accept the strains this overwhelming transformation may have on their relationship.

A woman expressed her deep love and deeply felt emotions during her labor and delivery:

• **"Joe was terrific—in the end I was far more thrilled at seeing Joe so happy than seeing the baby. (My maternal feelings were slow to develop, but steady.) This special closeness between us, I attribute to our preparation and the fact that Joe was there."**

A father describes his emotions:

• **"They left us alone for a time. We looked at our son. He was beautiful. I felt a sense of ecstasy, and a love and warmth for Sharon that was thick and palpable and alive. In my head, I kept seeing the birth, the body of my son emerging from Sharon's body. I didn't want to lose that image ever. The colors, the crying, Sharon's sounds of joy. We kissed and kissed again and looked at our son. What a woman, what a woman she is, I thought. And she is my wife and she loves me . . . and I, besides witnessing the majestic birth of my son, love Sharon more than ever."**

131

Postpartum

The period immediately following the birth is both exciting and complicated. It is filled with rapid changes taking place in the woman's physiology, but also with rapid changes taking place in the relationships within the family. The mother's body must go from its pregnant state to the non-pregnant state. That means her hormones must re-adjust and her blood supply must be reduced. Her uterus and vagina must return to normal size, her milk supply must either become established or be repressed, and her perineum must recover from any bruises or tears that have occurred during the birth. Even more overwhelmingly, both parents must get used to their new circumstance. Their relationship to each other and even to themselves will never be the same. Caring and loving emotions that might formerly have been shared with each other are now directed toward the baby, who seems to consume the mother's attention as s/he consumes the mother's milk. Fatigue caused by the work of childbirth, plus interrupted sleep patterns and an erratic nursing schedule tend to make the postpartum a difficult period for lovemaking, even for a couple who have stayed physically and emotionally close throughout pregnancy.

If sexual interest and response were related only to female hormones and steroids, then women would be uniformly disinterested in sexual activity until their ovaries resumed ovulation and steroid production sometime after the fourth or sixth week postpartum, the time generally recommended by doctors as a period of abstention from sexual intercourse. Nursing mothers might find that it takes them even longer, for suckling tends to repress the ovaries from producing either eggs or steroids. However, this is not always the case. Feelings at this time are very intense. They often include a special sense of excitement and physical intimacy between the new mother and father.

- **"Following delivery, I have found that I again have an increase in my desire for sex, especially the first week or so postpartum. It may for the most part be hormonal, but when I'm discharged from the hospital, I feel as though I've sprouted horns and my husband has to fight me off. I think that my not having seen my husband for a few days in the privacy of our own home, and also my again having a shape other than round contribute to this feeling."**

Emotional needs probably play a stronger role than physiology:

- **"One strain I had not totally anticipated was that when I was first home with our new baby, I needed physical closeness. I also wanted sex, but we were supposed to wait. The third day after birth—the day I returned home—we both felt a great passion and had a great "cuddle" in bed that night. "Cuddle" for us means orgasms for both of us, using my thighs. It got more difficult later on. My husband didn't want to try**

134

substitutes until I told him I just needed to be close. He started staying up late and I missed him in bed; he was waiting for a go-ahead from the doctor."

The change from the initial passion to a period of abstention for this couple might have been related in part to the dispersion of the vasocongestion and the appearance of the more typical picture of a nonovulating woman. But the fact that she could **tell** him what she needed, that is to say, his closeness, his tenderness and touch even without coitus was a great help to both of them and made it somewhat easier to get over the possibly strained period until the official all-clear was given. Masters and Johnson closely observed the sexual responses of six women during their postpartum period and found that their organs in fact did not respond as rapidly or as intensely as usual to sexual stimulation at their examination four to five weeks after giving birth.[18] Their responses had returned to normal at the examination conducted in the third postpartum month. During the period before the ovaries resumed ovulation, the vagina did not become as vasocongested or as lubricated, and these responses took longer to develop. Orgasms were shorter and weaker as measured by the researchers; the subjects did not report any significant difference in their orgasmic experiences. They enjoyed it as much at four weeks as they did at three months. Obviously, sexual responsiveness and pleasure are based on more than just physiology.

• **"We felt our lives changing for the better after the baby was born. Our sexual adjustment was**

gradual; it was really months before things were in a good and regular state, and it had more to do with a new openness and security with each other than with babies and birth. Certainly our growing respect and trust of each other as our child's parents helped in this direction—we had grown together."

Some couples pass quickly through this period of changed responsiveness. A lot depends simply on the amount of damage done to the woman's vagina by the baby's passage. If there has been an episiotomy or any tearing, it takes a while for the stitches to become comfortable. Bleeding from the uterus after giving birth is a normal and usual occurrence. It is called lochia, and is caused by the separation of the placenta or afterbirth from the inner wall of the uterus. Physicians generally give detailed instructions about specific body care postpartum and will explain that this bleeding will generally last about one month, though it often tapers off one to two weeks postpartum. This normal healing event may also hamper sexual activity. The doctor will give instructions to the couple on the time and when it may be safe to resume sexual activities, especially intercourse. Advice may vary considerably from case to case and physician to physician.

As the following accounts make clear, women vary a great deal in their experiences with sexuality after child birth.

• **"We resumed after three weeks the first time and about one to two weeks (as soon as I was comfortable) the second time. I think it is important that people know this, for many have**

136

been told to wait six weeks. I think this is much too conservative and should not be given out as a rule."

- "We had sexual activity up until the week I delivered and resumed it two weeks after our child's birth. During those two weeks I can't remember what happened, but my husband said we had oral sex on several occasions."

- "I feel because we practiced sex up until delivery and waited only three weeks after we didn't have the frustrations that a lot of couples—our friends—have when they must stop six weeks before and wait six weeks after. I feel we were both better equipped mentally and physically to adjust to the role of new parents. I felt sex during my pregnancy and the first few months after was the time we both needed it the most."

- "The postpartum period of abstinence passed almost without notice. Our lovemaking consisted of many, many things we did together that were not sexual, such as virtually holding our breath for every ounce the tiny, tiny fellow gained, exulting in every wrinkle that filled out to smooth cheek or chin or brow or buttock or calf or thigh."

Most couples describe having a greater or lesser degree of trouble with lovemaking in the postpartum period. For many it is simply the discomfort in the woman's vagina, a problem that can cause a great deal of concern at the time but which is usually worked out through patience and sensitivity between the partners if both truly desire intercourse.

• "After the birth, there was more of a problem about sex than during pregnancy. At first all of our time and energies went to the baby. But after about two weeks we both wanted very much to make love, and it was very painful for me. It wasn't completely comfortable until about three months postpartum, and many times I felt depressed—as though I'd been ruined by my baby, whom we'd both wanted so much and loved. Things improved steadily when I learned that all we needed to do was to give my vagina practice in stretching again. I really think more attention ought to be given to this. I've never talked about it to anyone, but I assumed I'd be back to normal within a few weeks."

• "We waited three weeks—it hurt! At the six-week check, my doctor told me that I'd feel better after my first period—which was true. My desire had increased immediately after pregnancy, while we were still abstaining."

• "After four weeks of abstention during pregnancy and five weeks after, sex was not as good as I had remembered. Physically, it was extremely uncomfortable, to the point of pain; emotionally, it was tragically disappointing. I was unprepared for these feelings, which made it even worse. After my first pregnancy, it took several months to disperse the tension associated with fear of pain and fear of not enjoying sex. I really never analyzed why it happened,

138

and wish I knew more about it. Perhaps women should be more prepared for discomforts, and increased knowledge by both doctor and patient could help."

• "I was exhausted during the postpartum period, though emotionally I felt very well. The baby was nursing eight to twelve times a day, and I was very sore from hemorrhoids. Despite this, I felt a strong reawakening of sexual feeling that I hadn't felt during pregnancy, as I remember. I was very anxious for the six-week checkup so we might resume. I was not at all prepared for the pain and discomfort of that examination, and for the first time, the diaphragm was difficult to insert. Intercourse, too, was painful for the first time. But this passed after the first few times, and my husband was patient and understanding. And now, though inserting the diaphragm is not as easy as it once was, I find I am getting even more sexual pleasure than prior to pregnancy."

These couples who feel a strong desire for intercourse but are surprised to find that it hurts could probably be helped by knowledge of the changed physiology. Especially when breastfeeding, the vagina is generally dryer than usual. It helps a great deal to use a lubricating jelly. It may be reassuring for a woman to know that she can respond, only that it will take her longer than usual because of hormonal changes. She may need extra cuddling, kissing and caressing to become aroused. But her body will be functioning normally within just a few more weeks. Couples who are eager to make love before the woman's body has

139

returned to its pre-pregnancy hormonal levels can usually enjoy sexual intercourse when they know these few facts. It may also be a good idea to let the woman be on top so that she can control the entrance of the penis. If her vagina is still dry, she will want to be careful.

Even when the baby has been delivered by Caesarean section and the vagina and cervix have not been through the trauma of birth, women discover that their sexual organs have been transformed by the experience. The same advice applies to couples following C-section as to those following vaginal delivery. There is the additional problem of abdominal discomfort getting in the way of relaxed and joyous lovemaking.

• **"Everything hurt after the section and my whole body was shot. I never realized that it would be like major surgery. It took me eight weeks before I could bear the idea of having sex, and having my husband on top of me really hurt. The doctor suggested we wait for six weeks, and I never expected to feel so rotten, because I am a strong person. I didn't know beforehand that it would be such a major thing for my body. Even now four months later, it hurts inside me, especially after my period. After ten weeks I was able to have an orgasm again.**

"I was very unprepared for all that. Nobody had told me about any of that beforehand. My husband was wonderful. He didn't seem to mind waiting. He didn't want to spoil anything by rushing into it and hurting me. He wanted to wait until I was really ready for it in order not to frighten me. After all we would have good sex

all our lives, and a few weeks didn't matter now. Even when the doctor gave us permission to have sex, my husband said, 'Let's wait another two days.' And I am glad, because then I was really ready."

• "I had complications after the section and when I came home I was exhausted. I didn't feel like making love at all. I felt torn between wanting to sleep and being with my husband. We started making love again about a month after the baby was born, though I felt like it much before. But my body felt too tired and bruised, or often the baby was crying. It didn't seem spontaneous anymore because of the baby crying so often. R. wasn't as understanding as he should have been. We had to work that out. He felt I should sleep during the day when the baby napped, and then be up with him in the evenings. But first my abdomen was hurting too much. That was for about two weeks, and then I was breastfeeding and that was a very sensuous experience for me, though I also wanted to be with R. Now it's three months later, things have gotten back together and now the baby is sleeping through the night."

• "My doctor said 'no sex' for six weeks. That didn't matter much to us as we don't feel it's so important to have penetration. But having had the baby, even though it was a section birth made me much more interested in sex and much more in contact with myself and my body. I found nursing makes one feel more in touch with oneself, like an animal with one's body. I had a tenderness in the vagina which lasted for a few months. But that didn't matter either, because we like other ways of pleasuring."

• "We were given the O.K. for sex four weeks postpartum. I almost died I was so uncomfortable. I was totally unprepared for such pain. The pain was inside my vagina. I breastfed and the doctor gave us lubricating jelly. That helped, but I had a vaginal irritation. We used other means of pleasuring like oral sex, but then I felt guilty about Richard and felt I had to take care of him too. There was certainly a strain about our new roles as parents. But after a little while we were careful. I did not want to beome afraid of sex, I felt that being tense once, I would be tense again and again. It took a few months until we were comfortable, though that was not due to the operation. We just had to schedule ourselves differently, like making love in the afternoons when the baby was asleep, at least on weekends. . .

A husband who is sensitive to the changes that have taken place in his wife's body may help make the return to intercourse easier.

• "We had discussed sexual activities with our doctor quite freely and he had given us free reign right through our pregnancy. In my eighth and ninth month of pregnancy I felt sexier than I had ever been in my life. That was great! After the section we waited for six weeks, mainly because of fatigue, and then the first time it hurt, plain physical pain. It felt like something was in the way. J. expected it to be difficult. He had

142

read somewhere that this was to be expected, and his attitude made it very easy for me. He knew that it was important not to do more than you can so as not to get frightened. So we did a lot of snuggling. The second time we tried, I felt much better and J. went in deeper. He did it very gently and stayed in a long time without moving too much and that felt good. I was on top of J. and that was important, because I could control the penetration. I made him come afterwards because I felt a little guilty, but J. was so gentle and said, 'be patient, don't push it.' I remember the feeling after the section birth: it was like being wounded when I was touched. And J. understood that. Strangely enough the vagina felt sore, especially at the front. I wonder why that is? I feel my whole body has changed and it feels good. I am in touch with J. and I am in touch with my own body now."

Sometimes fears and anxieties diminish the interest in making love:

• "After the birth I was quite uncomfortable and afraid of pain so we waited almost the full six weeks the doctor advised before resuming intercourse. During this time I worried that my vagina would not feel as good to my husband as it did prior to the birth and episiotomy. After resuming sex my husband kept reassuring me and in fact thinks I feel better now than before (probably thanks to the Kegel exercise)—a nice unexpected bonus."

The Kegel exercises are a good way to help woman's body return to good condition following a birth. Every woman has a strong muscle band arranged in a figure-of-eight reaching from near the pubic bone to close to the coccyx. Its name is the pubococcygeal muscle and its function is to support the bladder, the vagina, the uterus, and the rectum.

During pregnancy and birth the pubococcygeal muscle is exposed to strain from added weight and from being stretched during the delivery of the baby.

Unfortunately, many women are unaware of the importance of retaining good muscle tone in order to avoid a possible weakening of the pelvic floor, or even a prolapse in later life. Possible incontinence and a general weakness can be avoided by a good exercise routine during pregnancy and immediately after, and throughout life. Here's a description of the exercise which can be easily followed:

Sit comfortably, legs parallel and feet firmly on the ground

Tighten the front passage.

Tighten the vagina.

Tighten the back passage.

Hold, count to three.

Release.

The exercise can also be done standing or in the lying position.

Many women practice it while urinating, stopping the flow—counting to three—releasing it—repeating it two or three times.

A good way to involve one's partner in this is by squeezing the penis during coitus, thus enhancing the pleasure for both partners and also giving the husband a chance to tell whether the tone of the vaginal muscles has improved through frequent practice.

A father described his feelings after the birth of his baby:

• "I saw my baby born—I wouldn't have missed it for anything. But it took me a while afterwards to get used to the idea that this beautiful, warm, and dark vagina, which I had always thought of being there only for me, could also function in such a practical and overwhelming way. I had not thought of it before as a passageway for the birth of our little daughter. I really had to think this out and adjust to the idea—and making love to L. was difficult for a while. Once I accepted this dual purpose of the vagina, our lovemaking became as good as it had been before M. was born."

It is not unusual for a woman to simply be disinterested in sex for quite a long time following the baby's birth.

• "Our real problem came right after the baby was born and we were again able to have intercourse. For some reason I was unable for a few weeks to enjoy and desire sex. I believe that this problem could have become worse and lasted longer, but thank goodness I have a very patient husband and he did not push at all, but waited until I was ready."

145

- "After the baby was born I found that my desire for intercourse was greatly decreased for the first two months, which we attributed to being tired, sore, and because there was a great deal of intimacy (of a different sort, but nonetheless quite consuming) with the baby. Once back to work and with the baby sleeping through the night we both seem more anxious to resume our pre-pregnancy pattern."

Couples who actively resume making love together may find that the woman's responsiveness is mysteriously altered.

- "When we resumed our sexual activity there was definitely fear on both our parts: our fear of pregnancy which we hadn't had to worry about for the last nine months, my fear of being altogether (internally) again; and my husband's fear of hurting me. At this time I also think tensions are high because of a new family member and compounded by lack of sleep; and none of these things leads to complete enjoyment and fulfillment; but there was also a certain excitement again because there had been such a lapse of time."

- "Although we had made love since five weeks, until present (eight months later) I only achieved orgasm a week ago. I was a bit distressed during this period but not overly so because, though I never initiated sex, whenever we had it, I enjoyed it, though not to orgasm. My thoughts of why this has happened are that perhaps it is because my breastfeeding satisfied my emotional need for sex."

Frequently women seem to be so satisfied by their attachment to the baby that there is little need for other emotional ties. This is usually a very temporary fulfillment, which gives way to normal sexual satisfaction after a while. Nevertheless, it can place an unexpected strain on the marital relationship.

The postpartum contains more problems than just the successful re-establishment of sexual intercourse. One of the most conspicuous is the baby itself:

• **"Speaking for both my husband and myself, we felt the baby as an intruder. That seems such a hard word, but it accurately describes a baby. For the most part gone are those intimate moments of first awakening in the morning between husband and wife, if the baby awakens first, that is. And it is always possible the baby will want or need attention during intimate moments, quiet moments, exciting moments throughout the day or evening. The key (which I have not yet mastered) is to get back to those intimate moments after interruption, or to take advantage of other times."**

• **"My husband and I lead a fairly busy sex life though we've found that since the children were born sex sometimes has to take second place to a screaming baby."**

Not all couples see this as a problem:

• **"The baby has never been an intruder on our sexual life; she has caused us to plan a little more than before—but I don't think any more**

147

than certain methods of birth control do. She's always been a good and predictable sleeper, so has rarely interrupted us."

• "My doctor told us to wait for one month, which we did, but my husband was very impatient with this wait. I did not really want it before because my stomach was still so sore, though we used oral sex and manual pleasuring. But once I felt fine, we just resumed sex with the usual gusto. What I did find though was that relatives visiting were more of an impediment than the baby. The baby didn't disturb us much. It's a family joke with us now, 'Whatever happened to Love in the Afternoon?' Relatives, and the baby is awake."

• "In the early weeks after resuming sex, the baby herself did not intrude on our relations, but my exhaustion and discomfort did. The tenderness from the episiotomy lasted a good deal longer than six weeks and this surprised me. More importantly, my total absorption in the baby and mothering drastically cut my interest and desire for sex. After spending the day with a non-napping, non-stop baby and reassuring a sulking St. Bernard on hunger strikes, by evening I had absolutely nothing left to give. All I wanted was to be left alone, go to sleep or just regroup myself—to replenish the patient, love-giving attention I had used up during the day. At first I thought I was alone in this to the extent I felt it because I do tend to be a self-absorbed person. But friends have since told me that they felt the same—never watching as much mindless TV as they did from childbirth

148

to about three months. And I too found that midway through the third month I had integrated the baby into my life enough to return to a normal (and non-baby related) conversation and sex.

"The only problems now are fatigue and the pressure to get enough sleep early. I require a lot of sleep just to function rationally and unfortunately my daughter does not comprehend the idea of sleeping late on weekends. Consequently, Friday and Saturday nights are the same as all others—my non-stop day begins with the 7:20 nursing even when we've gone to sleep at 3:00 A.M. And it's never been found that fatigue aids sex.

"Paradoxically, in spite of fatigue and these other factors, sex has become much better for us since the baby. This is probably because we are now both much more patient with each other, because it is a release from the day's work, and, I think, because I feel so much more positively about my body and myself. A lovely unexpected dividend from our lovely baby!"

Nursing raises some special and interesting problems related to sexuality. It is in itself a sensual experience. A few women experience it as decidedly sexual; some have orgasms while nursing. Others direct their eroticism toward their husbands. This is slightly paradoxical. Nursing creates body changes; it causes the uterus to return to pre-pregnancy states more rapidly, but it also keeps estrogen and steroid levels altered longer because it tends to repress ovulation. This does not mean that breastfeeding prevents pregnancy. The chances are simply reduced. Similarly,

149

it does not **prevent** sexual responsiveness, but it does tend to inhibit lubrication.

● **"I feel that women who plan on nursing their babies should be told that during this period it is quite normal not to want sex or not to become turned on easily. It can cause a lot of bad feelings for the male and female involved if not told."**

A study of the biochemistry would make one suspect that nursing mothers, like the one just quoted, would want less sex. Yet in some studies, including Masters' and Johnson's, nursing women report being erotic sooner than non-nursing women, probably because the women in these studies who chose to nurse tended to be the women who felt more comfortable about using their bodies in an intimate relationship. The varying reponsiveness of nursing mothers to sexual arousal is another indication that body chemistry is not the only determinant of lovemaking.

In actual sex play, nursing breasts can be a joy or a handicap. They are large, but full. Arousal can cause them to leak or actually spurt great gushes of milk. Some couples love this, but others are turned off by it.

● **"As regards the effects of nursing, my milk tends to come down at the slightest touch to my breasts—and this is no tingle as the books suggest, but a real cramp and then the sheets are cold and wet."**

● **"Although I nursed, I never felt that it was in any way sexual for me. It brought me no particu-**

lar pleasure, but on the other hand wasn't an unpleasant obligation either. My husband couldn't really get off on the idea or the taste (he tried the milk once), so he didn't get involved sexually with my breasts. I suspect that I wouldn't have been interested either. I felt that one person using my nipples was enough."

• "Breast feeding I found indescribably beautiful and peaceful, though after about four months I was ready to give it up—demands on my time for one reason (my husband at the time was in bed with back problems and needed attention) and lactation during lovemaking after a while being an interference. I wanted my breasts to be for my husband and no longer for my child—our child."

Breast feeding may be the focus of a larger issue—can a woman love both her husband and her baby without feeling a conflict in her devotion to each of them?

A husband and wife pair have written intimate accounts of their postpartum adjustment from their two different points of view. First, the husband:

• "When we could finally think about such things as sex, we found that there was a difference. The difference was not especially disturbing to me. I recognized that we had naturally devoted a good deal of attention to lovemaking before, had actually focused on it because, throughout our several years together, it had remained remarkable, amazing, truly worthy of

151

focus and attention. Now, there was in both our lives and in our together-life a new factor not only very worthy of focus and concentration but irresistibly, insistently absorbing huge quantities of our libido.

"Our resumption of lovemaking began gradually and, somewhat to my surprise, remained gradual. I was still very interested (my wife is an incredibly attractive sexual partner), but not as interested as I had been before. Consequently I was also not as good a lover as I had been before. I did not feel that we had lost something extremely precious, but that its resumption was only deferred. Any anxieties I had stemmed from the fact that my wife had apparently been changed by the birth more than I had.

"She was definitely less interested in sex, and not only in terms of frequency. Some aspects of our foreplay, previously delighting, had become distasteful to her. My own diminished proficiency very likely contributed to her lessened drive. I am sure that she, like me, had a faint, almost but not quite unconscious suspicion that, when we made love, we were leaving our baby out, even though we knew intellectually that he would benefit from our success at the act of love. She required greater fastidiousness, both in herself and in me, cutting into the spontaneity.

"This matter came up in a weekly discussion group of young mothers, in which my wife is a regular participant. When she learned of the seeming universality of this phenomenon, she proposed that we sit down together and, as dispassionately as possible, talk the whole thing through. This we did, very recently and in our son's twentieth month it is producing positive results. I am doing some things differently and my wife is doing some things differently. We are coming back—perhaps even back to where our lovemaking used to be. Whether we achieve that ideal or not, we are re-experiencing the real joy of sex."

The wife speaks:

• "Unfortunately, the more I got into mothering, the less time/interest/desire I found for lovemaking. I was breast-feeding our son, and I was touching, holding and caressing him; being intimate with this tiny, helpless, beautiful being, I found my desire to hold, touch, and caress being met by my baby and really did not feel I wanted to be physically close to another person: my husband. Having been intimate with the baby all day, I found that when my husband came home and we put the baby down for the night, I needed time and space for myself. I also found that I was often exhausted by the end of the day—and now, almost two years later, as the mother of a very active toddler, I'm still tired.

"We found our sex life really falling apart. A great deal of this had to do with my getting adjusted to my new role as a mother—is a mother supposed to be sexy, relaxed, and abandoned in lovemaking? 'Of course,' you will say. 'A mother is still a woman.' I agree, but apparently this conflict of mother vs. sexy, to-

153

tally abandoned lovemaking partner was/is very deep in me.

"Some specific examples: (1) my husband had always enjoyed fondling and kissing my breasts, but while I was nursing (thirteen months) I didn't want him to have anything to do with the baby's 'territory;' (2) prior to my pregnancy, I had enjoyed cunnilingus, but now wanted nothing to do with it—perhaps this was a holdover from being told that we should not do it during pregnancy, or perhaps it was a newly developed feeling of fastidiousness, that I was somehow 'unclean' or that the act in itself was; (3) I found it difficult to relax enough to achieve orgasm—at the beginning perhaps this was a fear that we would be interrupted by the baby's awakening (although, as I recall, this never happened). It persisted, however, as the baby got older and his sleep patterns became more dependable; (4) I developed a fear of becoming pregnant again. It is too important to the development of our son that we not have another baby until he is at least three years old. All these factors added up to one hell of a postpartum sexual adjustment problem.

"We found ourselves making love much less frequently—once a week or every ten days as opposed to our prenatal average of three times a week. We found ourselves rationalizing that we had other interests now, were wrapped up in the baby, and that this was probably a normal development for all new parents. Perhaps it is quite common, but it was creating a lot of tension in our home. We finally admitted to each other that this was not a desirable situation,

154

and that we were losing a very precious and beautiful aspect of our relationship.

"We decided to open up the lines of communication, talked about the problem and now seem to be working it out. There is much less tension around here, my desire for my husband is returning, I want to make love almost as frequently as before, and sex is once again becoming an integral part of our marriage. As a result, I feel that we're much better parents for our son."

Summing Up

Our direct quotes have shown remarkably candid close-ups of situations common in marriage. For many women, the baby is a love object almost replacing the husband. Given the intensity of the mother-infant bond, particularly when the pair is nursing, this should not be surprising. In itself, it is not necessarily a problem. However, it can have disastrous consequences for the marital relationship. A family is a far more complex unit than a simple marital pair. After the addition of a new baby, the partners (but most particularly the woman, who is more biologically linked to the process) must work hard to maintain all the relationships that hold the family together. Parents must learn to embrace both their nurturant love for their child and their sexual love for their partner.

Some couples make this adjustment with ease. Others require months or years to work it out. Man and woman must remember to express their own love for each other even while they are taking care of a baby; for it is this love—the bond between mother and father—that holds together the family and creates a happy atmosphere for a child's growth. It also gives erotic pleasure and joy to the parents. The children are not the only ones in the family to have emotional needs.

Sexual behavior is an important index of a relationship. Intercourse is the physical union of male and female bodies. It is often described as a merger experience, a moment of total understanding, a profound coming together, a feeling of oneness. Conception is the most complete expression of this experience, for egg and sperm are literally two which become one. This is the ultimate biological union of male and female: the primal sex experience.

Men and women undergo profound personal, interpersonal, and social changes during pregnancy and the postpartum period. Lovers must add the roles of partner and parent to the way they interact with each other. They will never be the same again, alone, together, or in the eyes of the world. They may have to work hard to stay in touch with these changes in themselves and in their partner. Parenthood makes a shared life more complicated, but it also carries with it the potential to make life together more meaningful as lovemaking goes beyond caring for each other and spreads out to embrace the family unit.

• **"Susan and I feel that building our family helped us to reach toward sexual maturity. I know we had not reached it before we started on our family—perhaps we haven't even done so completely yet."**

Glossary

basal thermometer—A thermometer which shows 1/10 of a degree of Fahrenheit, as opposed to a regular fever thermometer which shows 2/10 of a degree. Used in determining period of ovulation in women.

Billings method—Method of birth control through detection of thickness of mucus discharge **during the period of ovulation.**

Braxon-Hicks contractions—Irregular and usually painless contractions of the uterus throughout pregnancy.

cervix—The neck of the womb.

coccyx—The tail bone of the spine.

crowning—The point at which the baby's head is visible at the opening of the vagina.

cunnilingus—The act of oral sexual activity (male to female).

dilation—The opening of the cervix during labor.

effleurage—A gentle massage over the abdomen, performed during labor contractions.

elevator exercise—Also known as "Kegel" exercise. A strengthening exercise of the pelvic floor and sphincter muscles to achieve good elasticity of the pelvic floor.

engorgement—Congestion of blood in tissues.

episiotomy—A small incision into the area between the vagina and the rectum to enlarge the vaginal opening during the birth of the baby's head.

gynecologist—A physician who takes care of women.

lactation—Production of milk in the breasts.

monilia—Fungus infection—in this case, of the vagina.

mucus plug—Mucus and small blood vessels, honeycombed, which form a plug in the cervical canal

obstetrician—A physician who takes care of pregnant women.

oxytocin—A synthetic hormone which will initiate labor.

postpartum—Generally the period of about six weeks after the birth of the baby.

prostaglandin—Substance found in the male prostate gland, which is believed to cause uterine contractions, but does not start labor in the concentrations normally found in human semen.

rhythm method—Method to determine the ovulation period in women by variations in temperature on waking. Determines safe and unsafe periods for intercourse with regard to fertilization.

steroid production—Hormones produced by the placenta (afterbirth) and ovaries to maintain and support normal pregnancies.

trimester, first—The first three months of pregnancy.

trimester, second—The middle three months of pregnancy.

trimester, third—The last three months of pregnancy.

uterus—The womb.

vasocongestion—Congestion of the blood vessels.

Notes

1. Marie Stopes, **Married Love: A New Contribution to the Solution of Sex Difficulties** (New York: Eugenics Publishing Co., 1930), p. 117.

2. Ibid., p. 118.

3. R. T. Trall, **Sexual Physiology: A Scientific and Popular Exposition of the Fundamental Problems in Sociology** (New York: Wood and Holbrook, 1877), p. 247.

4. Alex Comfort, **The Joy of Sex** (New York: Crown Publishers, 1972), p. 241.

5. William H. Masters and Virginia E. Johnson, **Human Sexual Response** (Boston: Little, Brown and Company, 1966).

6. James A. Kenny, "Pregnancy, Childbirth, and Breast Feeding as They Relate to the Sexuality of Women," **Human Sexuality,** May 1971.

7. Celia J. Falicov, "Sexual Adjustment During First Pregnancy and Postpartum." **American Journal of Obstetrics and Gynecology,** Dec. 1973, 117:991-1000.

8. For example, see Willy Pasini, "Sexuality during Pregnancy," **The Family.** Fourth International Congress of Psychosomatic Obstetrics and Gynecology, Tel Aviv, 1974 (Karger, Basel,

1975); J. Prochaska and A. Cernoch, "Coitus in Pregnancy," **Cesk. Gynek.** 35:282-87, 1970; and D. Bartova et al., "Sex Life During Pregnancy," **Cesk. Gynek.,** 34:560-62, 1969.

9. Don A. Solberg, Julius Butler, and Nathaniel Wagner, "Sexual Behavior in Pregnancy," **New England Journal of Medicine** 288:1098-1103, 1973.

10. Nathaniel N. Wagner, Ph.D. and Don A. Solberg, M.D., "Pregnancy and Sexuality," **Medical Aspects of Human Sexuality,** March 1974, pp. 53-54.

11. Celia J. Falicov, "Sexual Adjustment During First Pregnancy and Postpartum," p. 996.

12. Wagner and Solberg, "Pregnancy and Sexuality," p. 54.

13. Niles Newton, "Interrelationships Between Sexual Responsiveness, Birth, and Breast Feeding," in **Maternalism and Women's Sexuality,** pp. 77-98.

14. Masters and Johnson, **Human Sexual Response,** p. 135.

15. Newton, "Interrelationships," p. 96.

16. Sheila Kitzinger, **The Experience of Childbirth** (Baltimore: Penguin Books, 1970), p. 190.

17. "Dear Abby," **San Francisco Chronicle,** June 25, 1976.

18. Masters and Johnson, **Human Sexual Response,** p. 161-63.

ABOUT THE AUTHORS

ELISABETH BING, a member of the faculty of the department of OB-GYN of New York Medical College, was born in Berlin, Germany, of a distinguished scientific family. She was trained as a physical therapist in London, England, and came to New York in 1949. She worked under Dr. Alan Guttmacher in the Childbirth Education Program at Mount Sinai Hospital from 1952 until 1960. Elisabeth Bing became one of the co-founders of the American Society for Psychoprophylaxis in Obstetrics, Inc., in 1960. Since then she has continued her hospital work at the Flower and Fifth Avenue hospitals as instructor in childbirth education for the department of obstetrics and gynecology of the N.Y. Medical College. While continuing her hospital work, she has trained thousands of expectant parents in The Lamaze Method of Childbirth in her own private classes. She has traveled widely all over the U.S. and Europe, giving workshops, training childbirth instructors, lecturing and holding seminars in many colleges, hospitals and communities.

LIBBY COLMAN, Ph. D. is a young psychologist who, with her husband, Dr. Arthur D. Colman, is the author of 2 previous books, **Love and Ecstasy** and **Pregnancy: the Psychological Experience.** This book fills the long-felt need for an introduction to the psychological and emotional experiences which the pregnant woman and the expectant father will probably go through during the pregnancy. Libby Colman and Elisabeth Bing are personal as well as professional friends. The Colmans live in Sausalito, California, with their three children.